Mariana Borcoman

Scraps of Thought: Margin Notes in Old Romanian Books

PL ACADEMIC RESEARCH

Bibliographic Information published by the Deutsche Nationalbibliothek
The Deutsche Nationalbibliothek lists this publication in the Deutsche Nationalbibliografie; detailed bibliographic data is available in the internet at http://dnb.d-nb.de.

ISSN 0531-7320
ISBN 978-3-631-66046-1 (Print)
E-ISBN 978-3-653-05370-8 (E-Book)
DOI 10.3726/978-3-653-05370-8

PL Academic Research is an Imprint of Peter Lang GmbH.
Peter Lang – Frankfurt am Main · Bern · Bruxelles · New York · Oxford · Warszawa · Wien

This publication has been peer reviewed.

www.peterlang.com

Scraps of Thought: Margin Notes in Old Romanian Books

European University Studies

Europäische Hochschulschriften

Publications Universitaires Européennes

Series III	**History and Allied Studies**
Reihe III	Geschichte und ihre Hilfswissenschaften
Série III	Histoire et sciences auxiliaires

Volume/Band **1095**

Contents

Preface

Authors who wish to render events of the past using historical writings must have patience and the willingness to be objective. These two qualities along with my passion to search for testimonies of the past in the time-yellowed documents of the ages have guided the endeavor of this book. Old books and archive documents have marked my academic path for several decades. What I found in them sometimes surpassed my expectations. The years spent in the Faculty of History, University of Bucharest prepared me for this line of investigation.

This book was gleaned from the inventory of old books in the archive of the First Romanian School in Romanian Language established in Romania, in Şchei, a neighborhood of Braşov. That archive has 10,000 old books and documents. However, I focused on those belonging to the 17th century and thus the research narrowed down to only 42 books, 29 of which included margin notes, while the rest had no annotations whatsoever. These notes on old books, whether in manuscript or in printed form, are nothing but a few lines handwritten by those who ordered the book, received it or just held it in their hands for a while. They provide information such as book price (which equaled the price of several plots of land), measures to guard against theft (curses supposed to act as restraints on book thieves), its utility (for church service or for learning writing or reading in the school in Şchei) or its transfer from one person to another for reading purposes. All of the above are nothing but margin notes that in the 19th century are replaced by those made in diaries. Since the latter are private, they are part of a family's heritage and, regrettably, cannot be cited. Fortunately, the documents of the 18th century are available to researchers and bear notes that pertain to important political events (concerning Transylvania or the state powers around the province), issues related to the local community and its politics, regional Braşov weather incidents, vows to uphold moral behavior within the community or notes on the meetings of the priests from the Archbishopric of the Church of Saint Nicholas or from the churches nearby. Aside from testifying to events people considered important in their lives, margin notes can also be copies of older notes, which shows their role as a means of information transfer and dissemination. In this respect, what was considered of utmost relevance was recorded via these annotations!

The margin notes are also a testimony of a world that 400 years ago cherished handwritten or printed books and that was fully aware of their value and destiny to pass them on. Those who made notes were priests, cantors, copyists, deacons, squires, rulers or simple people who had had access to the books. The handwriting on book margins or next to the book spine impresses with its position, wording, sentence length (short or long) and the care taken not to interfere with the text itself.

As a result of my research I have unveiled a world inhabited by both officials of the Church or of the administration and by simple unknown people. Consequently, this book is also a chapter in the local history of Şchei, Braşov and in the history of mentalities.

The book is structured in four chapters:

CHAPTER 1: Introduction;

CHAPTER 2: Şchei, Braşov – a cultural center of Romanians;

CHAPTER 3: Margin notes in old Romanian books – a historical source;

CHAPTER 4: Şchei, Braşov – at the crossroads of Romanian aspirations.

In addition, it includes a chapter dedicated to conclusions, a bibliography and three appendices:

A. Catalogue of the 17th century books from the Şchei archive;

B. Names of the people recorded in the margin notes;

C. Alphabetical index of places mentioned in the annotations.

Last but not least, I would like to thank Dr. Vasile OLTEAN, the professor and priest who looks after the archive of the First School in Romanian Language in Şchei, Braşov, for his unreserved professional support.

October 12, 2014, Braşov, Romania

Chapter I. Introduction

1.1 Argumentative stance. An overview of research on old Romanian books

Old Romanian books are highly treasured artifacts that mirror Romanian spirituality and hence any research endeavor focusing on them needs to be understood within that framework.

First, the role and spread of printed and handwritten books must concern any research in the field of old books. On one hand, there is the printed form that required technical personnel and a printing press. On the other hand, there is the manuscript that entailed hours and hours of hard work on the blank pages.

Second, margin notes in old books are but one direction in the field of research. They are historical sources for dates and events that otherwise might be forgotten in the absence of other sources and which augment the picture of a past age. These notes introduce readers to the people who had access to the book by buying, donating or writing it. Researchers are able to acquire dates and information on people revolving around a cultural center. These brief annotations were made by owners who were fond of books and who took interest in the events around them.

The notes on book margins can render the image of an age. In this respect, their varied nature and contents provide information on book circulation, the community the book reached at a given moment in time, historical events or personal experiences (of rare beauty and distinction), or unusual weather phenomena that were closely related to people's preoccupations. When all this is placed and interpreted in the proper framework, the researcher restores the image of former mentalities. However, to understand these notes from a purely historical perspective is to dismiss much of our argumentative stance. Our interest is actually the people of the 17th century who recorded what they thought worth passing on to future generations in the prayer books that they dearly cherished. Therefore, it is difficult to identify the criteria by which the notes were made in the books.

The argumentative stance of this book focuses only on the margin notes made in the old books of the 17th century to be found in the archive of the First School in Romanian Language in Şchei. In this respect, the research aim is to take snapshots of the cultural center from the neighborhood of Braşov, as well as to introduce the people from Braşov and Bârsa County who took an interest in culture.

Old Romanian books as cultural monuments (similar in this respect to architectural monuments like churches or dwellings) unveil slices of life to researchers in the notes on their margins despite the evident respect the authors had for the book's text. Various researchers have focused on narrow territories and areas and on different historical periods by employing their own criteria. A chronological overview of these is presented below.

Nicolae Iorga is one of the prominent researchers who focused on old Romanian books and margin notes by undertaking research projects in several geographical areas known for their richness in such artefacts. The information on Braşov is gathered in his study published in Romanian in 1905 in Bucharest and entitled "Braşovul şi românii. Scrisori şi lămuriri" ("Braşov and the Romanians. Letters and Explanations"). This is included with another paper in Romanian entitled "Scrisori şi inscripţii ardelene şi maramureşene", ("Letters and Inscriptions from Ardeal and Maramureş"), published in 1906 in "Studies and Documents on Romanian History" (unless otherwise indicated the publications cited here were originally published in Romanian). The latter provides information on circulation of books and points out that most of the books in Transylvania came from "Ţara Românească" (Wallachia). Other works by the same researcher are: "Inscriptions from Romania's Churches" dated 1905–1908 which is a complex work, and "Inscriptions and Annotations From the Churches in Iaşi", dated 1907, Bucharest. In his "Observaţii şi probleme bănăţene" ("Observations and Issues from Banat"), the great historian also paid particular attention to the 18th century Romanian books from the Banat area. This was published in 1940 in Bucharest and focused on the annotations from several printed documents (some of which are attributed to Nicolae Stoica from Haţeg).

Ioan Bârlea, an apprentice of Iorga, takes his mentor's advice and publishes his work on the identification of the origin and path taken by old Romanian books. Moreover, by reproducing their margin notes he provides information on book price, socio-historical contexts, relationships among the areas from Maramureş, as well as on the two Romanian provinces – Moldova and Wallachia. This information is contained in his book *Însemnările din bisericile Maramureşului* ("Annotations from the Churches in Maramureş") dated 1909, Bucharest.

In 1938 Dariu Pop undertakes his research in the same field as Bârlea in the Satu Mare area and publishes *Mărturii strămoşeşti. Note din cărţile bisericeşti sătmărene* ("Ancient Evidence. Annotations in the Churches From the Satu Mare Area").

P.P. Panaitescu conducted a study on the old books from the archives of Timişoara city that was published in "Revista istorică" (Romanian for "History Magazine") of 1922 under the title of *Însemnări din cărţile bisericeşti româneşti (greco-orientale)din Timişoara* ("*Margin notes in the Romanian (Greek and Oriental) Church Books of Timişoara*"). His aim was to simply render the annotations as such.

G.T. Kirileanu made an important contribution to the field by concentrating his research efforts on the Piatra Neamţ area. Hence, in 1923, he published in the *Convorbiri literare* magazine ("Literary Conversations") a study entitled *Însemnări istorice pe cărţi vechi bisericeşti din Buhuşi-Neamţ* (*Historical Margin Notes in the Old Church Books from Buhuşi-Neamţ*). As its title suggests, the latter concentrated on the annotations found in the archive of the Buhuşi- Neamţ church which had been founded by the Buhuş Toader family. In addition, he also studied the old book archives of the town of Focşani and published the findings in the local magazine *Milcovia* between 1931–1932. He focused on the margin notes in the books dated from the 17th, 18th and 19th centuries. According to his conclusions, the margin notes in the old books are a good record of their ownership, as well as of events like Turkish invasions, the politics of the rulers from Wallachia in relation to the Ottoman Empire, earthquakes, droughts, etc. Moreover, they highlight the perception of books value by unveiling deeds and disputes among heirs for their ownership.

During the inter-war period, the researcher Valeriu Literat conducted studies in Ţara Oltului (Olt County), an area with many historical resources. The work he published in 1938 under the title of *Din Ţara Oltului. Însemnări vechi din biserici noi* (*Old Margin Notes from New Churches in the Olt County)* provides a list of the books from the churches in the above mentioned area, as a well as a chronological presentation of their margin notes.

Biserci vechi din lemn din Ardeal ("Old Wooden Churches from Ardeal") by Athanasie Popa is a book broader in scope compared to the ones mentioned because, by focusing on the margin notes in the books, it also highlights their value.

The Bihor area is covered by the research conducted by Tit Roşu in 30 residential areas and published in *Însemnări şi inscripţii bihorene* ("Margin Notes and Annotations from Bihor") in 1941. Nicoale Liu in his study *Cartea cu insemnări manuscrise* ("Books with Handwritten Margin Notes") included in the volume Studii şi cercetări de documente şi bibliografie (*"Studies and Research on Documents and Bibliography"*) and dated 1967 emphasizes that if the margin notes providing book ownership details were arranged chronologically they would supply highly useful information concerning the areas where Romanian books had spread. Moreover, referring to the curse to be found in some of the margin notes he interpreted it as a sign of the owner's sense of property and affection for the book.

Ioana- Cristache Panait researched the old books from the wooden and stone churches in Lipova and Buziaş, as well as their margin notes. The study she published in "Mitropolia Banatului" (Romanian for "The Ecclesiastical Metropolis of Banat") is dated 1969 and known under the title of *Cărţi vechi cu însemnări din bisericile Mitropoliei Banatului* ("Old Books with Margin Notes from the Churches within the Ecclesiastical Metropolis of Banat"). Liviu Patachi, in his turn, concentrated on the Haţeg County and published *Cărţi vechi religioase din Ţara Haţegului peo listă întocmită în 1867* ("A List of Old Religious Books from the Haţeg County dated 1867") in 1968.

I.C. Chiriţimia studied the spread and circulation of books from Wallachia and Moldova to Transylvania. His findings were issued in *Mitropolia Olteniei* ("The Ecclesiastical Metropolis of Oltenia") in 1970 as *Din vechea răspândire a cărţilor româneşti în Transilvania* ("On the Old Circulation of Romanian Books in Transylvania"). Octavian Şchiau published the article *Circulaţia cazaniei lui Varlaam în Transilvania* ("The Circulation of Varlaam's Homily in Transylvania"), which included important stories related to the aforementioned book, in the same magazine and in the same year as Chiriţimia. Moreover, he also concentrated on analyzing categories of book readers and emphasized that the readers of books in the Romanian language were the priests and the educators.

Dan Rîpă- Budiu is another researcher contributing to the studies on the archives of old books in Romanian language from the churches belonging to the Lower Danube Episcopacy from Galaţi. He published a study in the "Danubius" journal issued by the history museum of Galaţi from 1972–1973. After having organized the margin notes chronologically and transcribing them in accordance with modern phonetic methods (especially for autographs and curses that are highly relevant for the plasticity of the language), he analyzed them and found information on book price, local craftsmen and book readers.

Ilie Corpus made another important contribution to the research field of margin notes in books. In "Annotations of Yore" dated 1975, Bucharest, he outlined the margin notes found in the archived manuscripts of the Romanian Academy and was the first to structure them by categories as follows:

- Internal political issues;
- Wars, foreign occupation and invasions;
- Legal, administrative, social and economic history;
- Weather forecasts and their influence on agriculture and the market;
- Floods;
- Locust invasions, epizooties, epidemics;
- Education;
- Book price and circulation;
- Fires, earthquakes;
- Eclipses and comets, as well as a chapter on local events.

Florian Dudaş conducted a study on books in the Romanian language in the Bihor area. His findings were published in Oradea in 1977 as *Carte veche românească din Bihor*, (Romanian for "Old Romanian Books from Bihor") and record the presence in the archives of Oradea city of single copies of two books: *Evangheliarul românesc* ("The Gospel Book in the Romanian Language") printed by Coresi in Braşov in 1561, and *Psaltire românească*, ("The Psaltry in the Romanian Language") printed by the same scholar in Braşov in 1570. The old books in the Almaj Valley area were studied by Valeriu Leu who notes the special treatment of these books as precious objects whose bindings were therefore refurbished. His analysis of the causes for book scarcity in Banat in the 18th century was published under the title of *Circulaţia cărţii româneşti în valea Almăjului până la 1840* ("The Circulation of Romanian Books in the Almaj Valley until 1840") in "Banatica", a publication issued by the Caraş- Severin County Museum, in 1979.

The researcher Eva Mârza scrutinized the Olt Valley. She compiled a catalogue of the books in Romanian language found in the parish libraries and presented her conclusions in an article titled *Cărţi româneşti pe valea Gălzii* ("Romanian Books from the Gălza Valley"), issued in "Apulum", Alba Iulia, 1979.

The above mentioned magazine hosted a study on the book archives from the village churches in the Sebeş Valley authored by Drăghicescu Doina between 1981 and1982.

A team of researchers from the Romanian Academy assembled by Ioan Bianu, Nerva Hodoş and Dan Simonescu compiled a three volume book called "*Bibliografia românească veche*" ("Old Romanian Bibliography") the majority of titles of old books in the Romanian language dating back to the 15th, 17th and 18th centuries. Another volume was added later by Dan Simonescu. Barbu Teodorescu's book *Cartea veche românească 1508–1830* ("The Old Romanian Books between *1508–1830")* is an overview that focuses on the books printed in Bucharest, as well as of the evolution of printing.

In his book *Aria de răspândire a cărţilor de Râmnic în Banat în secolul al 18th-lea* (*"The circulation of the books printed in Râmnic in Banat in the 18th century"*) Virgil Molin records the distribution of the books printed in Râmnic and highlights the role these played as church cultural guides. Dimitrei Coravu analyzes the phenomenon of book circulation from Moldova and Muntenia to Transylvania despite the constraints imposed by the Austrians in the 18th century in *Aspecte ale activităţii de tipărire şi răspândire a cărţilor bisericeşti în Transilvania,Muntenia şi Moldova* ("Features of church book printing and distribution in Transylvania, Muntenia and Moldova"*)*.

All of the above studies enrich the research efforts directed towards the old books in the Romanian language by presenting specific geographical areas and novel information on the books, as well as on their margin notes. Besides these, there are two books of a more general nature, namely *Biserica ortodoxă română una şi aceeiaşi din toate timpurile* ("The Romanian Orthodox Church – an Everlasting Undivided Entity") by Nicolae Bălan, the Metropolitan of Ardeal, published in Sibiu in 1980, and *Legăturile bisericeşti române ortodoxe din Transilvania cu Ţara Românească şi Moldova ăn sec. XVI-18th* ("The relationship of the Romanian Orthodox Church from Ardeal with Wallachia and Moldova between the 16th and 18th centuries") written by Professor Dr. Mircea Păcurariu and published in Sibiu in 1968.

Nicolae Bălan, the Metropolitan, underscores the importance played by old printed books for the Romanians everywhere and singles out the awareness of the printers from Muntenia and Moldova that book printing in the Romanian language was a necessity for their brothers from Transylvania. Thus, as his research shows, the books printed in the two regions were more often than not destined for the people in Transylvania. His book also presents a list of the old books from several large residential areas: Alba, Braşov, Mureş, Sibiu.

In his turn, Mircea Păcurariu provides evidence that the books in the Romanian language were an intrinsic part of the cultural relations among the three Romanian regions. Moreover, he outlines the means by which books were distributed.

1.2 An outline of sources

a. Unedited sources

This book draws on the margin notes written in the old books from the 17th century to be found in the archive of the First School in Romanian Language in Şchei, Braşov. Most of the material has never been published and the transcripts of the Cyrillic or Slavic texts belonging to Professor Dr. Vasile Oltean were edited and added to serve the goal of this book. Some of these transcripts were first made public by Mr. Oltean in some of his works: *Şcoala românească din Şcheii Braşovului ("The School in the Romanian Language in Şchei, Braşov")*, Bucharest 1989, and *Întâia şcoală românească din Şcheii Braşovului* ("The First School in the Romanian Language in Şchei, Braşov"), Braşov 1981, as well as in some of his articles published in the literary publication "Astra" from Braşov.

For all of the above I would like to express my deepest appreciation and to thank Professor Fr. Dr. Vasile Oltean.

As far as the sources used for this book, they are part of the books from the inventory of the Museum of the First School in Romanian Language, an inventory that can be consulted and is very well preserved. There are 46 books from the 17th century but not all of them contain margin notes. The contents of the margin notes can be found in the appendices of this book. Additionally, the appendices also include the lists of people's names that are mentioned in the margin notes and an alphabetical index of places mentioned in book annotations. In order to better organize the information on these books and margin notes, besides a standard description chart (including book title, inventory number, size, book binding type), I used a personal call number system ranging from 1 to 29. In the cases when two books are bound together the call number is followed by a volume letter, a and b.

As for the work titles, I strove to maintain the original titles by consulting the existing documents referencing them and the inventory in Şchei. The call number system from 1 to 29 reflects the chronological order of the books. Above the call number, I also recorded the language in which the book was written. When a work mentioned fully in the appendix is referenced in the book, its call number is used. The criteria by which I used to focus on the margin notes in the old books were identified while I studied them.

Besides the works consulted for this book and those inventoried in Şchei between the 17th and 19th centuries, the archive also contains material that cannot be consulted given its poor preservation and the absence of title and contents pages. Until measures to preserve and restore are taken this material cannot be properly used. What is more, some material from the inventory has perished (mostly due to fires).

b. Edited sources

One of the edited historical sources that this book builds upon is *Cronica popii Vasile din Şcheii Braşovului* ("The Chronicle of Priest Vasile of Şchei, Braşov"). Even though its original version has not been preserved, a part of it is still available in the German language. Besides that, I also consulted the work of Radu Tempea *Istoria Sfintei bisearici a Şcheilor Braşovului* ("The History of the Holy Church in Şchei, Braşov") edited by Sterie Stinghe under the same title in 1899. A more thorough edition of this book that is closer to the orthography used today was edited by Octavian Şchiau and Livia Bot in 1969. Tempea's chronicle covers an extended time period from 1484–1742. For the 1484–1659 time period Tempea relied on the original version of the old chronicle of Vasile, the priest, by transcribing it almost entirely. For the 1659–1742 time period, the researcher used a series of documents, records, lists of Orthodox deceased found in the well-endowed archive of **the Church of Saint Nicholas** in Şchei, Braşov, as well as dates and events he had witnessed or compiled from old priests. The work is dedicated to the activity of the priests and cantors in Şchei and to the permanent cultural relations they had established and built with Moldova and Wallachia. The work emphasizes that the Orthodox Church in Şchei was not isolated by the Catholic pressures. On the contrary, it was fully supported by the Church in the two Romanian regions in various ways. In this respect, the neighborhood of Şchei itself played a salient role in the multiple relations established between Braşov and Wallachia during the 16th and 17th centuries and it was protected by Wallachia and Moldova as an important cultural center. Up to 1700 the chronicle records the changing of priests, cantors, deacons, administrators of church goods, as well as the disputes among priests. As of 1720, Radu Tempea becomes a prominent character of his chronicle, and hence the latter records events of his life triggered by his relationships with the Romanian community in Şchei. The reactions of the Romanians from Braşov to the propaganda around the idea of unifying the three Romanian regions (Transylvania, Wallachia and Moldova) and to their dependency on the Saxons were triggered by the aspirations of the wealthy people in Şchei which, up to a point, were shared by the entire Orthodox community.

Tempea presents sufficient arguments in favor of viewing Şchei, the Romanian neighborhood of Braşov, as a bastion for the ancient Orthodox faith.

Information on the chronicle of Vasile, the priest in Şchei, Braşov can be found in the documents hosted by the Saxon archive of the city in **Quellen zur Geschichte der Stadt Kronstadt**. These were published in a seven volume book that, besides records of expenses, accounts, debts, contains lists of current expenses made for the repair of the citadel and its fortifications, documents dated between 1503 and1550 and belonging to the University of the Saxons. The fifth volume of this compilation, which includes chronicles and diaries, dedicates some of its first pages to the chronicle of Vasile, the priest in Şchei.

The picture of the age under scrutiny in this book is completed by the documents edited by Sterie Stinge and published under the title **Documente privitoare la trecutul românilor din Şchei (Documents on the past of the Romanians in Şchei)** in Braşov in 1901. The two-volume work covers the time period between 1700 and1783 and is compiled based on a selection of the documents found in the archive in Şchei, Braşov. It presents a number of arguments supporting the actions of the Orthodox Romanians in Şchei, as well as the latter's correspondence with the rulers and high officials of the Orthodox Church from Wallachia.

Chapter II. Şchei, Braşov – A Cultural center of Romanians

2.1 The Church of Saint Nicholas and the School in Şchei

The school in Şchei was established and run under the patronage of the Church of Saint Nicholas from the same neighborhood of Braşov. Consequently, the goal of this chapter is to provide an overview of the people who served before and during the 17th century in the two institutions. In order to do this, it will outline a cultural micro-monograph of Şchei by highlighting the contribution and development of the Şchei school of copyists.

First, the chapter will briefly provide some information on Şchei, as a neighborhood of Braşov, and on the Church of Saint Nicholas.

The Romanian community in Şchei dates back long before the establishment of the Saxons in the region. Initially, the citadel of Brassovia is raised by the Teutons on the Tâmpa Mountain and Şchei lies to the West of the citadel. The town of Braşov is first mentioned in 1252 in a decree of King Bela IV. In 1292 the Bulgarians inhabit the south of the city. There are vivid debates concerning the place of origin of the latter. Most scientists support the idea that the term 'Bulgarian' is used by Saxon documents not to refer to the homonymous ethnic group but to the Vlachs. The latter come from the Southern Carpathians and merge with the Romanian community in the area. Today their generic name is *şcheieni*, a name derived from the name of the neighborhood they inhabit, namely Şchei. With the arrival of the Saxons in the Bârsa County in the 13th century, the Romanian community becomes subordinated to the German administration of Braşov.

The Romanian community in Şchei makes its living from raising animals, cultivating their land (that was rather barren) and trading. Their habit of exhibiting their merchandise in wooden 'troci' ('troughs') (troughs were also used as instruments to which small hammers were attached in order to manufacture chenille) earns them the nickname of *'trocari'*, *"a nickname by which people from outside Şchei would use for the inhabitants from this neighborhood"*[1].

---

1 Constantin Lacea, *Trocar,* in "Ţara Bârsei" (Romanian for 'The Bârsa County'), May-June 1931, no. 3, pp. 234–237.

The Romanian community in Şchei is economically independent, but is administrated by the Saxon authorities. This community was of Orthodox religion and, hence, felt the need to raise a church. Since the Saxons were Catholics and unlikely to support them in such an endeavor, the community asked for support from their 'brothers' in faith and ethnicity from Wallachia. The latter not only supported the building of the church, but also its later activities. Initially, it was built of wood in 1300, with a priest and a cantor serving it. One person worth mentioning for this beginning is Vlad Călugărul, the first Wallachian ruler to sponsor the church. However, his name is no longer recorded by the List of the Deceased that identifies all those who have made a contribution to the church (In this respect, Muşlea emphasizes that the initial List of the Deceased has been lost). The wooden church was situated to the left of the current stone church and initially dedicated to the Virgin Mary's Dormition. Later on, the church was named after Saint Nicholas of Myra, the miracle worker. It was in this wooden church that Laiotă Basarab was buried.

There is a lot of information on the history of the Church of Saint Nicholas in Şchei. Both the Romanian community and the activities of church representatives must have been pretty influential and perceived as a threat by the Catholics. Consequently, in December 1399, Pope Boniface IX issued a bull by which the Catholics (namely the Saxons) from Braşov are urged to take action against the 'heretics' on the border of Corona (another name for Braşov).

The chronicle of the church written by protopope Vasile mentions the first priest named Pătru in 1484. However, in 1477, in Neagoe Basarab's writings there is a mention of a priest named Costea who travels as a messenger to Wallachia. As for Pătru, his son succeeds him as a priest and that marks the beginning of a long list of priests and school teachers in Şchei about whom there is information that they wrote letters in the Romanian language for the Chancery of the Saxon University from Sibiu. Concerning this, the son of Pătru is actually requested by the magistrate of Braşov to perform such services.

The history of the school of copyists in Şchei, Braşov covers three periods:

A. School and church establishment;
B. The Coresi period when the school in Şchei becomes a well-known cultural center;
C. The 17th century Humanism along with the 18th century Enlightenment.

The decision to build a stone church next to the wooden one is motivated by two factors: the number of community members outgrows the size of the wooden church, and the economic power of the merchants in Şchei is on the rise. In addition, the church chronicle mentions a terrible plague in Braşov around 1495. Consequently, in order to escape the plague, the residents of Şchei make the decision to build a stone church. To achieve this goal, the community asks Neagoe Basarab, the Wallachian ruler for support. He donates large sums of money and it seems that he becomes involved to such an extent that apparently the church "is built according to his plans"[2]. At the same time, a school to meet the needs of the children from this neighborhood is also established. For this age, the number of educated people is quite limited and, as a result, priests act as teachers as well. Consequently, the activities of this school cannot be separated from those of the church.

2.2 Priests and school teachers

Apart from priests who also act as teachers, there are people whose work is solely related to school activities. They are called Chancery secretaries and their responsibilities are to draw up documents, write correspondence or to lecture. The first such person is known by the name of Gheorghe (1492–1497), but there is not much information on him. Along with him, there is another secretary, Radu, who accompanies the priest Coman (a contemporary of priest Petru) as a messenger in Wallachia and decides to settle there to serve the ruler of that time, Vlad Călugărul (1481–1484). Acting as messengers on behalf of the Saxon Council was a common and lucrative responsibility for the priests and cantors in Şchei.

2 Prişcu Ioan, *Vechimea bisericii Sfântu Nicolae din Şcheii Braşovului (Romanian for The Fustiness of Saint Nicholas Church from Şchei, Braşov)*, in "Ţara Bârsei" (Romanian for 'The Bârsa County'), July-August 1931, no. 4, p. 339.

The documents of town magistrate record these trips and provide information on various persons who conducted their activities in Şchei. Moreover, as a result of their knowledge of both Romanian and German languages, the priests and school teachers were paid to act as translators for the officials of Braşov.

By the beginning of the XVI century, the relationships between Şchei and the other two Romanian regions, Wallachia and Moldova, flourish. In the context of the preparations made for Coresi's arrival in Braşov, the school teachers in Şchei travel across the mountains quite often. In this respect, a number of Chancery secretaries stand out as messengers dispatching messages in Şchei to the Wallachian rulers before Coresi's coming to Braşov. They are Oprea, a Chancery secretary (1536–1545), acting as messenger to the Wallachian ruler, Radu Paisie (1535–1545); Nan, also referred to as *logofăt*[3], and Costea who are also known for the messages they communicated to the administration of Mircea Ciobanul in Wallachia in 1545.

Educational responsibilities are shared not only by priests and Chancery secretaries, but also by school teachers. Some of the latter's names are recorded to this day. Stoica Dobromir is one of these educators who also acts as Chancery secretary between 1530–1580, as well as a messenger to the Wallachian rulers Petru Rareş and Vald Călugărul and to Rucăr and Sibiu on behalf of the Saxons from Braşov. Apart from his role as a messenger recorded in **Quellen zur Geschichte der Kronstadt**, there is very little information on his activities. Other educators are: Stoican, who is also sent on a diplomatic mission to Vlad Înecatul in August 1530; Stanislav, whose name is mentioned in the correspondence between Radu cel Mare (Radu the Great) and Christian, a functionary from Braşov. Last but not least, there is also Sava, who comes to Braşov with a letter of recommendation and money from Alexandru Lăpuşneanu, ruler of Moldova: "The stay of this representative of Lăpuşneanu in Braşov can be related to the Moldavian's ruler donation in 1560 of an impressive **Tetraevangheliar** (The Four Gospels) with miniatures and written on sheepskin by

3 A position characteristic for Middle Ages Wallachia and Moldova that referred to a high dignitary from within the hierarchy of boyards who also acted as a councilor to the ruler.

Mateiaş Logofătul"[4]. Apparently, Sava decides not to return to Moldova after Lăpuşneanu is overthrown.

This ongoing exchange of messages between Braşov and the Romanian rulers from Wallachia and Moldova takes place both officially, on behalf of the Saxon magistrate, and informally, as a means to obtain support for the school and church in Şchei that contributes to forging cultural relationships. The support on behalf of the Romanian rulers from across the mountains consists of financial donations and valuable books that can be still found in the archive in Şchei to day. These written artifacts are used for a twofold purpose: for religious and educational reasons. In this respect, the evidence can be found in the margin notes made in these books by those who used them to learn reading and writing or by those who wanted to become priests and educators.

Before Coresi's arrival in Braşov, deacon Oprea works with protopope Mihail and is the figure whose activity is well known in the field covered by this book. In this respect, in 1579 he transcribes an **Octoih românesc (The Romanian Octoechos)** translated long before in 1544. Most likely this deacon is the same as Coresi's collaborator, Oprea – the *logofăt*, who is both "a craftsman and a school educator for the apprentices who take courses to become educators"[5]. This piece of information is representative for school course offering: an elementary course on basic knowledge for everyday use, and an advanced course in Greek and Latin offered to future school educators and priests. School activities unfold in the wooden church, but soon it becomes too small for the increasing number of students.

All of the above along with the arrival in Şchei of Mihai, priest and protopope, open a flourishing period for this neighborhood of Braşov. Mihai, son of Dobre, a descendant of an old family in Şchei that goes back to the priest known by the name of Pâtru cel Bâtrân (Pâtru the Elderly) is active between 1578–1604, focusing on:

- The church and the Orthodox believers in Şchei;
- The school and the young students course attendees;

4 Oltean Vasile, *Şcoala românească din Şcheii Braşovului (Romanian for "The School in the Romanian Language from Şchei, Braşov")*, Bucureşti, 1989, p. 20.

5 Ibidem, p. 39.

- Copying books in the Romanian language. In this respect, it is worth noting that before Coresi's arrival in Braşov there is already a well-established school of copyists that uses the Romanian language.

Much as his predecessors did, Mihai acts as a messenger to the Moldavian ruler, Aron Vodă, on behalf of the church in Şchei. Consequently, he receives 12,000 Turkish silver coins that he uses to build up pillars in front of the church and a brick building, larger and better organized, for school related activities. The same priest is mentioned by the chronicle written by his son, Vasile, as the one who meets Mihai Viteazul (Michael the Brave) upon his entering Braşov and asks the latter to spare the villages from the Bârsa County. During his time, the church in Şchei reaches its maximum development as a result of the numerous annual donations and valuables. In this respect, it is worth mentioning that the church owns land and includes a neighborhood, and land across the mountains from donations made by the Romanian rulers, like the donation of the Micşuneşti estate made by the son of Michael the Brave, Nicoale Pătraşcu, and his spouse, Voica in 1602. The church is surrounded by a high stone wall with cells hosting monks, school educators, Chancery secretaries, as well as rulers and their female relatives from across the mountains passing through Braşov or taking refuge in Şchei from their enemies.

When the church was first established, the religious service was held by one priest and a deacon. With its increase in scope and size, the church becomes the protopope's residence and hence, there are two or three priests serving in it. Moreover, the church in Şchei extends its jurisdiction over most of the Romanian churches from the Bârsa County. Concerning the efforts to surround the school with a wall, protopope Mihai, has to overcome the challenges raised by authorities, as well as resource scarcity. The plot of land used to raise a new school is bought for 18 florins by the protopope who personally "endows the school with books so that its activities can unfold properly and uses his education for school progress"[6].

This is the time when several important representatives of the school and church in Şchei translate and copy books in the Romanian language,

6 Ibidem, p. 56.

act as messengers and make efforts to build the new school. One such figure is the priest Dobre (1541–1572), father of protopope Mihai and who is justly called a scholar by his nephew. He not only dispatches message to the rulers from Wallachia and Moldova, namely Petru Rareş and Alexandru Lăpuşneanu, in 1544 and 1568, but he also purchases two manuscripts from the priest Bratu that he binds and donates to the school in Şchei. Other important personalities of the time are the deacon Oprea, whose activity has already been mentioned, the priest Voicu (1572–1578) who also acts as a copyist and as a result of his efforts in this field copies the Slavonic version of **Învăţăturile morale din vieţile sfinţilor** (**Moral Teachings of the Saints' Lives**). Another important person of the time active at the same time as protopope Mihai is the priest Iane (1575–1591), who along with Mihai translates Coresi's **Cazania** a II a (**Homily II**). His presence and activity as a copyist within the school of copyists in Şchei are recorded by a letter in the Romanian language written upon the request of Lukas Hirscher, a functionary from Braşov, which mentions the intentions of some boyards from Făgăraş County to intercede in the matter of the killing of a Saxon from Săcele and the wounding of some residents of the Church of Saint Nicholas from Mândra.

In conclusion, the school teachers, priests and copyists in Şchei play an important role in preparing the ground for Coresi's arrival and activity in Braşov. The latter establishes the printing press in Şchei and not in Braşov, despite his initial collaboration with the functionary from Braşov. The manuscripts copied in Şchei are to be well used by Coresi in his printing activities and, in this respect, the priests from the neighborhood work closely with him. As far as Coresi's printed books are concerned, Chapter III will offer more details.

The end of Coresi's activity in Braşov coincides with the end of the 17th century and the beginning of the 18th century, an age characterized by great uncertainties for Wallachia, Moldova and Transylvania resulting from the death of Michael the Brave and the collapse of his idea of a union of the three. One major change that occurs is that Transylvania is no longer an autonomous principality under Ottoman rule but a province subordinated to the Habsburg Empire. However, neither the Turks, nor the Austrians are able to break the old relationships established by Braşov with Wallachia and Moldova. In this respect, this town can be viewed as a hub of merchants who keep the Romanian spirit alive and offer refuge to the rulers and boyards from across the mountains. Even when the Romanian Church United with Rome, that is the Greek Catholic, is established, the Orthodox in Şchei maintain their faith. However, the 17th century is a troubled one for the activities of the church in Şchei. The latter is well organized and wealthy, but it is undermined by the fights among its priests that also require that community members to take sides. Consequently, this lack of consensus and homogeneity at a community level allows for the pressures on behalf of the Saxon authorities to take effect. The Saxons are keen on appointing the priests in Şchei and in this respect a covert network of hidden agendas related to the Romanian Orthodox parishes emerges. However, despite this involvement on behalf of the Saxons, the practice of nominating the priests serving in the Church of Saint Nicholas from within this neighborhood of Braşov is a well-established one. One particular case that supports this hypothesis is that of the priest Neagoslav Munteanul who comes to Şchei from Târgul de Floci, Moldova upon the advice of Michael the Brave. However, in 1606 he is removed from his service on the grounds that he is not a local. In this respect, some priests and school teachers who serve in the two establishments in Şchei are from well-known families in Şchei. As far as the administration of the church is concerned, some changes occur which concern the appointment of church administrators whose role is to supervise priests.

The people working for the church and school in Şchei struggle to preserve the values of the previous century. Nonetheless, this period is one less favorable for strengthening Romanian culture due to the political situation of Transylvania, the interferences on behalf of the rulers from across the mountains and the repeated invasions of the Turks.

Some of those who choose to become priests also make the choice of acting as scholars and thus continue the legacy of the school of copyists in Şchei. To mention them here is to pay them their dues given the troubled times they had to endure. One of these whose activity is worth mentioning is Vasile, the chronicler (1586–1659), son of protopope Mihai. He is raised and educated to love and respect books and holy teachings and as a result of this he writes *Cronica bisericii Sfântu Nicolae din Şcheii Braşovului* (The Chronicle of the Church of Saint Nicholas in Şchei, Braşov) that covers the time period that starts with 1292 –the moment when the *bolgari* settle in Braşov – and continues for the whole duration of his activity with the school in Şchei. The original chronicle in the Romanian language is lost, and the only one that is preserved is the German version. Moreover, Radu Tempea's work *Istoria Sfintei besearici a Şcheilor Braşovului* (The History of the Holy Church in Şchei, Braşov) mentions it. This chronicle does not include too much information on the neighboring areas of Şchei since its main goal is to describe the activity of the priests in Şchei: ***To outline priests' work and appointments in this church, beginning with the priest Pătru the Elderly and continuing until the times of the priest Constantin, as well as their struggle and endeavors to preserve the church and its legacy unaltered.***

Another important work of Vasile the chronicler, is *Parâmierul românesc* (*Romanian Chant Book for Lent*). It not only informs us about his activity as a copyist and translator, but it also documents him as "being the first Romanian chronicler who goes far beyond the scope of old analysts who simply record isolated data and events"[7](for more information on this see the appendices).

In the second half of the 17th century, a conflict over the nomination as priests of the Church of Saint Nicholas between Ioan, son of a wealthy merchant in Şchei named Florea Corbea, and Staicu Hoban emerges. In order to settle it, they are sent to be ordained in Wallachia and afterwards appointed as priests in Şchei along with Radu Boilă, a priest who is already serving in the Church of Saint Nicholas. In the last decades of the 17th century, priest Vâlcu raises claims for a priest position with the church. To this end, he addresses the town magistrate and the Metropolitan of Ardeal, Sava Brancovici. Finally, he obtains his appointment with the Church of Saint Nicholas and serves here along with three other priests: Staicul, Oprea, Văsii, son of Comşa Răuţ from Tohan. In 1686 Vasile Grid is appointed priest in Şchei, Braşov. During this time period, the trips to Moscow continue with a view to supporting the activities of the Orthodox Church in Şchei. In this respect, it is worth mentioning the visit of protopope Vasile Hoban in 1697.

7 Aurel A. Mureşianu, *Un dascăl braşovean necunoscut în veacul XVII* (Romanian for An Unknown School Teacher from Braşov), in "Tara Bârsei" (Romania for The Bârsa County), November-December 1931, no. 6, p. 200.

The legacy of priest Vasile is taken over by the school educators Costea, Giurcă, Cârstea, Andrei, as well as by Alexandru Polonul and Petru Şoanu. The school educator Costea (1689–1704) is a translator of widely circulated books of popular wisdom. One of his manuscripts that belonged to a family of school educators from Şchei by the name of Radu Cătană can be found in the archive of the Romanian Academy and includes the following writings: *Gromovnic* (a book of forecasts on human fate and weather phenomena depending on the correlation between thunders and lightning and the time period of the signs of the Zodiac), *Floarea darurilor* (The Sum of Virtues), the oldest translation of Fiziologul (a compilation of stories in which the main characters are animals representing vices and virtues), Cosmografia (The Cosmography), a Cronograf (Chrongraph, a handbook of world history) and Legendele Sibilei (The Legends of Sybil).

Alexandru Polonul (1690–1700), from Liov, translates and copies books for didactical purposes. Some of his works are: Penticostarul (Romanian for The Pentecostarion) a translation of a Slavonic printed book dated 1694, Mântuirea păcătoşilor (The Sinners' Redemption) translated from Greek and Patericul (a collection of stories about the lives of those declared saints by the Orthodox church) of the Pacerska monastery from Kiev.

Concerning the school educator by the name of Giurcă, the information is scarce. "He is mentioned in a document dated 1700 from the Făgăraş archive – a letter of the functionary from Braşov addressed to the commandant of the citadel of Făgăraş that presents the results of the investigation on the inheritance of the two daughters of Giurcă, a school teacher from Braşov"[8].

Petre Şoanu (1706–1741), school teacher and priest, authors the first calendar in the Romanian literature by relying solely on his own means. Two copies of this can still be found in the Library of the Romanian Academy.

As far as Costea is concerned, it is his signature on a Minei (Romanian for Menaion) dated 1681 that unveils his family origins as the son of the priest Staicu and his status as school teacher. Information on the activity of Ioan Cărăuş, mentioned by Radu Tempea's chronicle, is just as scarce. In 1712 he is ordained in Wallachia by Antim Ivireanul, the Metropolitan.

---

8 Vasile Olteanu, *Şcoala de copişti din Şchei (Romanian for The school of Copiysts from Şchei),* in "Astra", 1980, no. 4, p. 12.

Even though the above mentioned school teachers are very much in the background, they play an important role in the transition towards Enlightenment when education becomes secularized.

The above chronological information is but one way of understanding the contribution made by the school of copyists in Şchei, Braşov to the preservation and development of the Romanian language and culture. In this respect, before focusing on the most important families of scholars from Braşov, it is worth understanding the type of books that are transcribed by the above mentioned copyists.

According to Vasile Oltean, the school of copyists in Şchei "dates back to the 11th century, at the same time with an Omiliar (Collection of Homilies) which is proof that education was done orally through religious sermons"[9]. This hypothesis is supported by a number of religious books found in the library of protopope Mihai: Carte folosoitoare de suflet-Cuvântările lui Efrem Siriul (Spiritual Growth- The Sermons of Ephrem the Syrian) (manuscript 13 in the Şchei archive), as well as Lesavicinic-Scara Sfântului Ioan (Saint John's Ladder of Divine Ascent) (manuscript 17 in the Şchei archive).

The first stage in the history and typology of these books is characterized by their religious scope when they are used for training priests in the art of giving sermons.

During the second stage hagiographic books emerge aimed at familiarizing readers with saints' lives and offering moral guidance. A representative book in this respect is a "Sinaxar (Romania for Synaxarion), written before 1477 by priest Costea in Şchei, a scholar well known for his relationships with Wallachia"[10].

The third stage is completely dedicated to hagiographic books with religious and moral contents, some of which are: Învăţăturile morale din vieţile sfinţilor (Moral Teachings from Saints' Lives), written by priest Voicu, and Cuvântări de sfinţi şi pilde de folos sufletesc (Saints' Sermons and Parables for Spiritual Growth), signed by Onofrei Costevin from Calicia.

---

9 Ibidem, p. 13.

10 Vasile Oltean, *Şcoala românească din Şcheii Braşovului (Romanian for "The School in the Romanian Language from Şchei, Braşov")*, Bucureşti, 1989, p. 79.

The fourth stage dates back to the 15th and 16th centuries and is shaped by the personality of the priest Bratu (1490–1515). The representative documents for this period are letters in the Romanian language dated 1495 and two books titled Molitvelnic (The Book of Common Prayer).

The last and most important stage between the 17th and 19th centuries is shaped by the influence of prominent families of scholars like the Hobans (1598–1700), the Bărans (1650–19th century), the Grids (1721–19th century), the Corbeas (1690–the 18th century), the Temeas (1678 up to 1850) and the Dumas (1740–the 19th century). More information on these families is provided below, as well as in the appendices.

1. The Hoban Family

The members of this family that are representative for the goals of this book belong to the second lineage of Stanciu Hoban (1613–1634), who lived on Tocile and worked as a school teacher in Şchei. His son, Vasile Hoban I, is known for his work as a school teacher and copyist, while Vasile Hoban II (son of Vasile Hoban I) is the first school teacher in Şchei and appointed protopope of the Church of Saint Nicholas. The last descendant of this family, Barbu Hoban, is also a school teacher near the end of the 17th century.

2. The Băran Family

The first member for whom there information is Florea Băran. He comes from a family of merchants in Şchei and works as a school teacher and priest as of 1692 and later as protopope. He authors the "first documents in the Romanian Cyrillic alphabet". The son of Florea, Teodor Băran, attends the courses delivered in the Şchei school and completes his education in Râmnic and Câmpulung. His attitude concerning the resistance of the Orthodox Romanians from the Bârsa County against the Union with the Roman Catholic Church led by the protopopes in Şchei is not a clear-cut one. One reason for his ambiguous approach to the above mentioned issue is the conflict he has with Radu Tempea II over his appointment as priest in the church in Şchei. After making a complaint at Viena against Tempea, Băran is reinstated as priest in 1736. Vasile Băran is the second descendent of the family and he is mentioned as working as a school teacher in 1734. Moreover, as mentioned by a margin note made in a Romanian language handbook, there is also a Ioan Băran, acting as a school teacher in 1831.

3. The Grid Family

Protopope Vasile Grid (1686–1747) comes to Şchei from Făgăraş and along with Radu Tempea II supports the cause of the Orthodox Romanians by travelling on a regular basis to Vienna in order to denounce Saxon pressures. He has two sons: Eustatie Grid (1721–1767) and Jipa. The latter, however, converts to the Greek Catholic faith and, as Tempea mentions in his chronicle, is appointed for a while protopope of the Romanian Greek Catholic from Braşov. The statistics from the archives of Braşov indicate Eustatie Grid as the richest priest from Braşov and the Bârsa County. He dies in 1764 at the age of 64. Dimitrie Eustatievici, son of Eustatie Grid (1730–1796) is an important figure for the educational environment from Ardeal and authors *Gramatica românească* (The Grammar of the Romanian Language), dedicated to Constantin Mavrocordat, the ruler. Muşlea Candid lists the descendants of the Grids as follows: Eustatie Grid has a son by the name of Dimitrie and four daughters, Ilinca, married to Radu Cătană; Anastasia married to Zamfir Marcu; Paraschiva widow of Stan Munteanu and Maria, widow of Dinu Gheorgiuceanu from Giurgiu; Gheorghe, the hierodeacon, 1722 (son of Florea Grid, the priest); Petru Grid, the hierodeacon; priest Oprea Grid from Râşnov, 1723; Petru Iosif Grid priest and school teacher; protopope Petru Grid, 1777; priest Dimitrie Grid, 1779; and last but not least the hierodeacon Nicolae Grid who completes his education in Cluj and then teaches in the school on Tocile in 1813. The latter authors the chronicle of Şchei for the period from 1383–1813, a chronicle that is later continued to 1861 by Voinea Pitiş and Dimitrie Orghidan.

4. The Corbea Family

The chronicle of the Church of Saint Nicholas mentions the name of Florea Corbea, son of Ioan Corbea, school teacher and diplomat in 1659. Ioan has three sons, David, Teodor, also known as Pătru, and Matei. He becomes a monk in the Sinaia monastery and takes the name of Joseph. David Corbea, the youngest son, studies in Kiev until he is contacted by Constantin Brâncoveanu, the Wallachian ruler and becomes a diplomat in his administration. He takes the side of the Orthodox Romanians from Braşov in the religious conflict they have with Metropolitan Athanasie Anghel. Along with Nicolae Milescu, he settles in Russia in 1723 upon the request of Peter the Great. He dies in Varsaw and is buried in Kiev. His brother, Teodor Corbea, is hired as secretary in the Chancery of Brâncoveanu in 1698. After the battle from Stănileşti in 1711, Teodor and Toma Cantacuzino, the sword bearer, go to Russia where the former spends the rest of his life. In the Chancery of Moscow he works as a translator.

5. The Tempea Family

There are at least six descendants of this family for whom information is available.

Apparently "the ancestors of this family crossed from Oltenia or Wallachia to Ardeal and settled in the Făgăraş area from where, at the end of the 17th century, some of the family members came to Braşov, while others headed for Banat"[11]. The first name of all family members is Radu and therefore they are difficult to tell apart without distinctive features of their activity. Radu Tempea I is (?–1713) is asked by Vasile Grid to come from Făgăraş in 1699 and act as a priest and school teacher in Şchei.

Radu Tempea II, the chronicler (1691–1742), takes the courses conducted by the school in Şchei, and then continues his education in Râmnic and Câmpulung. He authors the chronicle of the church in Şchei.

Radu Tempea IV (1741–1743), is educated at the school in Şchei to become a school teacher and then a priest, and marries Marina, daughter of a merchant from Şchei by the name of Oprea Floroiu.

Radu Tempea V (1768–1824) is also called the Chancery writer because of his activities in this field. He publishes a grammar textbook used in the pedagogical school from Braşov that he ran as a director. He gets his degrees from the school in Şchei, the Lutheran grammar school from Braşov and then from Buda as a result of the sponsorship he gets from the church and community of Şchei.

Radu Tempea VI (1796–1850) is known as a rector in Vâlcea and also for his dedication to education. In 1814 he begins his work as school teacher in Şchei, continues as a deacon in the the Church of Saint Nicholas and then moves to Râmnicu Vâlcea.

---

11 Candid Muşlea, *O dinastie de preoţi şi protopopi Radu Tempea (Romanian for Radu Tempea: A Dynasty of Priests and Protopopes)*, Bucureşti, 1939, pp. 6–7.

6. The Duma family

This family apparently "comes from the Ottoman Empire"[12], or "from somewhere around Banat or Făgăraş"[13].

The first Duma representative is a church administrator who, together with Radu Tempea II, participates in the actions of the people in Şchei against the Union with the Roman Catholic Church. He is joined by his son, Dimitrie Duma, who is a deputy of the prior, as well as church administrator. He dies in 1775 during a plague epidemic in Braşov. Ioan Duma, son of Dimitrie, is a school educator in Şchei in 1758. He takes music classes, acquires theological knowledge and Greek language skills in Bucureşti. He translates and copies books for school use and is also skilled in poetry. Radu Duma II, the school teacher, continues the chronicle of Radu Tempea II after 1742 under the pseudonym of *Simerian Hiară*. Moreoevr he plans to write another chronicle and to translate the Mineie (The Menaions) into Romanian. The last descendent of this family, Nicolae Duma works as a school teacher in Şchei during the reign of Maria Theresa.

All of the above are portraits of people devoted to Romanian books and culture and who act as models for their contemporaries by inculcating in their souls the passion for the written word. Additionally, they are still models even nowadays as a result of their work for their descendants' future. This is how the collective mentality is actually preserved.

---

12 Idem, *O dinastie de preoţi şi protopopi Radu Tempea (Romanian for Radu Tempea: A Dynasty of Priests and Protopopes)*, 1939, pp. 6–7.

13 Vasile Oltean, *Şcoala românească din Şcheii Braşovului (Romanian for "The School in the Romanian Language from Şchei, Braşov")*, Bucureşti, 1989, p. 90.

Chapter III. Margin notes in Old books – A Historical source

3.1 Features of Old Romanian books: The Manuscript and the Printed Book

To focus on the margin notes made in old Romanian books first requires some additional information on this category of books and on the history of the printing press and typographies in the three Romanian countries of the 17th century: Transylvania, Moldova and Wallachia.

Correspondence written in Romanian dates before manuscripts transcribed in the same language begin circulating. For the latter, a certain level of language stylization is required and that can only be attained by employing writing for daily needs and commercial transactions.

In this respect, it is worth mentioning that in the 1495 financial accounts of Sibiu, a town in Transylvania, there is a mention of a priest by the name of Pătru who worked in Brașov and was employed by the administration of Sibiu for his proficient writing skills in the Romanian language. Moreover, the letter of Neacșu dated 1521 and addressed to Johann Benkner, a dignitary/functionary[14] from Brașov, is masterfully penned. The employment of the Romanian language in writing is facilitated by the increasing number of daily needs, while Slavonic is still the language used in official documents and in conducting the Orthodox Liturgy.

All of the above are characteristic of the 17th century and unveil the struggles and disputes on using the Romanian Cyrillic alphabet in favor of Slavonic in writing and printing. This is a time when the printing of religious books in Romanian is a strenuous endeavor since there are religious norms and canons forbidding that. The first texts that are translated into Romanian and disseminated through manuscripts are books targeting common people, or destined for reading as a leisure time activity, or for spiritual enlightenment.

---

14 '*jude*', Romanian for a dignitary in charge of administrative and legal responsibilities.

In terms of collective mentality, all of the above highlight the emergence of a group of readers able to understand these writings and to use and further disseminate them. Even if nowadays it may seem all too natural, such a development could not have been a spontaneous one. It is actually the outcome of a change in people's consciousness resulting from perceiving reading as a need. This transformation process is obviously linked to the 15th century political events from Wallachia which helped to create a buffer zone for Transylvania between the Ottoman Empire in the South and the great Christian powers in the West.

Additionally, the economic development that characterizes the end of the 15th century and the beginning of the 16th century leads to changes that contribute to the emergence of an urban bourgeoisie. Compared to the feudal class, this newly formed group has a completely different lifestyle that involves writing and reading as essential activities. Moreover, the preferences of the newly formed bourgeoisie are for secular books which are copied for personal use.

Additionally, a new generation of learned people emerges and its goal is to revive cultural values by proceeding from religious books. As a result, the translation of these books is heavily influenced by the above mentioned factors. The work of this generation is facilitated by the appearance of the printing press and its spread throughout Europe in general and in Transylvania in the fifth decade of the 16th and 17th centuries. However, there are difficulties in printing books in the Romanian language because of the monopoly and censorship of the Church in this field.

Thus, the first books in the Romanian language are actually manuscripts (from the study on Coresi's activity) that actually contribute to heavily molding the defining features of the Romanian language. The first printed work in the Romanian language is the *Calvinistic Catechism,* issued in Sibiu, in 1544 and edited by the a typographer Filip Moldoveanul. The book is meant to serve political purposes and to persuade the large number of Orthodox Romanians from Transylvania to convert to Calvinism.

As of 1535 Honterus establishes a typography in Braşov to serve the needs of the Saxon authorities in the area and beyond. Moreover, in 1532, Johann Fuchs şi Johann opens a paper mill for commercial purposes. That is actually what prompts Coresi to come to Braşov and, since his plans serve economic interests, the Saxon authorities are more than willing to accept them. In addition, the Romanian community in Şchei, Braşov, plays an important role in establishing and maintaining relations of various kinds with the Romanians from Moldova and Wallachia. The Saxons are interested in honing these connections and, consequently, they recruit their chancellors and secretaries, as well messengers to dispatch their missives across the mountains from within this community. In this respect, P.P. Panaitescu notes the following on the above mentioned Romanian community: "The Romanian neighborhood of Şchei plays an important role in the multiple relationships established between Braşov and Wallachia beginning with the 16th century. As such, it was a wealthy center protected by Moldova and Wallachia, and the Romanian Orthodox Community that inhabited it took an interest in the commercial, diplomatic and religious liaisons among the three Romanian countries"[15].

Last but not the least, the school in Şchei hosts a constellation of scholars, priests and cantors who not only write in the Romanian language, but also support such endeavors. Hence, the works printed by Coresi are written in a language crafted by the priests in Şchei. In this respect, the researcher Nicolae Sulică emphasizes: "Coresi had not been concerned before with issues of a linguistic nature or related to writing in the Romanian language. The solutions to these were the sum of a collective effort of generations of translators and interpreters who had striven to establish a coherent writing style and a literary language"[16].

Related to all of the above it is worth mentioning that an invisible network of relations among the people in Şchei is supported by the school and church from this neighborhood so that the priests are recruited from among the former cantors and secretaries in the Chancery (who also act as chanters and deacons) to later become protopopes. Traditions like erudition are passed on from father to son. Usually, if there are more sons in

15 Petre P. Panaitescu (1960) *Începuturile scrisului în limba română* (Romanian for *The inception of writings in the Romanian Language)* in "Studii şi articole de istorie medie" (Romanian for: "Studies and articles on Middle Ages History"), IV, pp. 150–185.

16 Nicoale Sulică (1943) *Minunata cetate a Braşovului-cărturari braşoveni aisecolului al XVI-lea, ca ctitori ai limbii noastre literare* (Romanian for *The Wonderful Citadel of Braşov – scholars of the 16th centuries from Braşov and their role in establishing the Romanian literary language)*, Braşov, p. 11.

a family, the elder is educated to become a priest and after the death of his father he takes over the priesthood for the church in Şchei. The other children in the family are also educated to make contributions to the community. When referring to the reason that made Coresi choose Braşov and discussing the role played by this scholar, Mircea Păcurariu states the following: "Braşov used to be the center of the cultural revolution of those times, a center at the crossroads of Romanian interests"[17].

Deacon Coresi was an apprentice in the printing workshop of Dimitrie Liubovici from Târgovişte. When he comes to Braşov he brings with him, as his aide, a Chancery secretary by the name of Oprea. The deacon's activity can be divided in several stages:

1. 1559–1565: he associates with Hans Benkner, the functionary, for editorial purposes who then orders Coresi to print books in Romanian and in Slavonic.
2. 1565- Coresi associates with the Hungarian noble, Forö Miklos (a promoter of Calvinism in Transylvania) for a few months.
3. After 1567, Coresi starts acting as an editor on his own. As of this moment, the printing of books in Slavonic and Romanian is sponsored by the rulers and metropolitans of Wallachia.

The books printed by Coresi are as follows in chronological order: 1559 – Întrebarea creştinească (The Christian Subject), the first book Coresi edited that is dedicated to Efrem, the metropolitan of Ungrovlahia (that is Wallachia or "Wallachia near Hungary"); Zbornicul[18] slavonesc (The Slavonic Corpus) published between 1568–1569 and Octoihul[19] slavonesc (The Slavonic Octoechos) issued between 1574–1575, commissioned by

17 Mircea Păcurariu (1968) *Legăturile bisericii ortodoxe din Transilvania cu Ţara Românească şi Moldova în secolul XVI–XVIII)* (Romanian for *The Relations of the Orthodox Church from Transylvania with Wallachia and Moldova between the 16–18th centuries)*,Sibiu, p. 103.

18 t.n.*'zbornic'in old Romanian stands for a corpus of.*

19 t.n. 'octoih' in Romanian refers to the fundamental Orthodox collection of chants in eight byzantine tones used for the weekly Service; also referred to as 'Octoechos' or the 'Book of Eight Tones'.

Alexandru II[20] (1574–1577) and Mihnea Turcitul[21] (1577–1583); Evanghelia cu învăţătură (The Gospel and Its Precepts) (1581) published with the support of Metropolitan Serafim of Ungrovlahia and with the collaboration of priests Iane and Mihai; Liturghierul slavon (The Slavonic Liturgical Book) commissioned by Mihnea Vodă and issued in 1588.

Coresi is joined in Braşov by two apprentices, Mihai and Mănăilă, by the above mentioned Chancery secretary, Oprea, and by his own son, Şerban Coresi. The latter participates in the publication of the book known by the name of Palia[22] (old Romanian Pentateuch or The Five Books of Moses) from Orăştie. Radu Tempea's chronicle mentions Coresi's activity in Braşov briefly, but it emphasizes the gains obtained by the priests in Şchei from printed books: "...during the time of Herjel Lucaci, a good Christian and dignitary from the citadel of Braşov, and of these priests from Şchei a lot of books in Romanian and Serbian languages were published ... and these priests managed to increase the number of books for the church"[23].

The language used in the books published by Coresi is actually a mix between the language spoken in Northern Muntenia and Southern Transylvania.

Coresi's contribution is but one stage in the history of printing books in the Romanian language. In this respect, external unfavorable constraints influence the next stage in this history. Consequently, book printing in the Romanian language stalls until its further development by Matei Basarab[24] and Vasile Lupu[25], once they come to power. Thus, a third stage in the history of book printing in the Romanian language is recorded at the end of

20 t.n. Alexandru II Mircea, ruler of Wallachia between 1568–1574 and 1574–1577 and father of Mihnea Turcitul.

21 t.n. Mihnea Turcitul, ruler of Wallachia between 1577–1583 and 1585–1591. He is known for his burdensome fiscal policy that was applied to privileged categories to meet the Turkish requirements for resources and to remove Petru Cercel, his competitor, from rule. Upon his relegation in 1591 he converted to Islam and hence was nicknamed 'Turcitul', that is 'the one who accepted the Turkish faith'.

22 t.n. the oldest translation of the Old Testament published at Orăştie in 1582.

23 Radu Tempea (1969) *Istoria Sfintei besearici a Şcheilo Braşovului* (Romanian for *The History of the Holy Church from Şchei, Braşov*), Bucureşti, p. 59.

24 t.n Ruler of Wallachia between 1632–1654.

25 t.n.Ruler of Moldova between 1634–1653.

the 17th century and beginning of the 18th century. Its main figures are: Varlaaam, Dosoftei[26], Antim Ivireanul[27] and Mitrofan. Book printing in the Romanian language becomes widely spread between 1716–1780 and the printing facilities of Bucureşti, Rîmnic, Buzău, Rădăuţi, Blaj are used constantly.

The books printed during the reign of Vasile Lupu and Matei Basarab are actually "an ideological weapon for administrative and religious authorities, as well as a means to counter the Catholic and Protestant Reformation propaganda. Printing activities were under church monopoly and were subsidized by rulers or by the Orthodox Church"[28].

Matei Basarab[29], under the guidance of his cultural advisor, Udrişte Năsturel[30] decides to introduce the printing press in Wallachia and, to this end, addresses a letter to Petru Movilă, the Metropolitan of Kiev. Petru Movilă sends him a printing press that is installed under the supervision of Timotei Verbinţki in Câmpulung. At the same time, a press managed by Meletie Macedoneanul is running at Govora. This is moved afterwards to the Dealu monastery and later on to Târgovişte. Moreover, Ocnele Mari hosts a paper mill. Vasile Lupu, in his turn, receives a printing press that is installed in Iaşi, within the precincts of the 'Trei Ierarhi' monastery and under the supervision of Sofronie Paceaţki.

In parallel with the above mentioned presses from Moldova and Wallachia, a printing press is running in Bălgrad.

---

26 t.n. Metropolitans of Molodova (Varlaam was appointed Metropolitan in 1632 and with the support of Vasile Lupu, ruler of Moldova at the time, establishes the first printing press in this country. Dosoftei was a Metropolitan begnning with 1671).

27 t.n. Metropolitan of Wallachia between1708–1716 who founded a new printing press in Târgovişte. He is believed to have first learned the craft of printing in Moldova and then from Mitrofan (former bishop of Huşi) in Bucharest and upon the latter's appointment as Bishop of Buzău, takes over operations and continues printing religious books.

28 Mircea Tomescu (1968) *Istoria cărţii româneşti de la începuturi pănâ la 1918* (Romanian for *The History of Books in the Romanian Language from its beginning until 1918*), Bucureşti, p. 65.

29 t.n. ruler of Walachia between 1632–1654.

30 t.n. brother-in-law of Matei Basarab, as well as a scholar, translator and poem writer.

A comparative outlook on the books printed in Moldova and Wallachia highlights differences in terms of the language used. As a result of Vasile Lupu's and Varlaam's liberal approach, the religious books printed in Moldova are in the Romanian language, whereas those issued in Wallachia during the reign of Matei Basarab are still printed in Slavonic. Related to that, it is worth reminding that, geographically speaking, Wallachia is much closer to Transylvania. Hence, Slavonic is viewed as the means by which to counter the pressures exerted by Catholic representatives, to promote the use of Romanian language in school and in church and thus, to maintain the Orthodox tradition.

In the second half of the 17th century, the printing activities are resumed with the efforts of educated priests who come from among common people. Such examples are Metropolitan Dosoftei, who writes to the Patriarch of Moscow requiring support for endowing the printing press from Moldova, and who also takes an active stance towards introducing the Romanian language in the Orthodox Church, as well as Varlaam, who establishes printing in Bucharest in 1678 during the reign of Şerban Cantacuzino. During the rule of Șerban Cantacuzino and Constantin Brâncoveanu in Wallachia, the activities related to printing and writing in the Romanian language flourish. Consequently, in 1682 the Evangheliar (The Gospel Book) is issued in the Romanian language, while the Bible in the same language is printed in 1688.

Constantin Brâncoveanu, the Wallachian ruler, plays a major role in Romanian culture. He sends young people on scholarships abroad, runs a well-organized Chancery and is in permanent contact with the representatives of the Orthodox Church. In this respect, he operates several printing presses with advice from Metropolitan Antim Ivireanul, as follows: in Snagov (1696), in Râmnicu Vâlcea (1708), in Târgovişte (1709), in the Antim monastery (1716) and in Buzău under the supervision of Bishop Mitrofan (as of 1691). What is more, during the administration of Brâncoveanu, there is also a printing press that prints books in Greek. Brâncoveanu's endeavor to publish books in the language spoken by the common people, Romanian, is nothing but a means to counter the pressures made by the Catholics and to shield the Orthodox faith from any reformation attempts.

The establishment of the printing press in Râmnic is part of an ingenious plan on behalf of the high priests from Wallachia to actually make up for the scarcity of books in the Romanian language from Transylvania and thus support the Orthodox church in this area to confront the difficulties caused by the Reformation among others. Consequently, the books printed in Wallachia become widely spread in Transylvania in the first decades of the 17th century.

The evolution of the printing press and of manuscripts during the 18th century is covered by well documented papers in the field and is not the research aim of the current endeavor. However, there is one thing worth noting since it sheds light on the area of concern for this book. There is one valiant attempt on behalf of a person by the name of Petcu Şoanu to build a printing press by exclusively relying on personal means. The output consisted in a number of calendars. In this respect, Tempea notes the following in his chronicle: "1731. Petcu Şoanul, the cantor, started to do printing even though he had not seen how to do that anywhere whatsoever, and printed some calendars that included information related to the signs, forecasts on birth dates and future phenomena, all of which came from sources he had taken from the priest Statie. Nonetheless, the Orthodox church does not acknowledge such foreknowledge"[31]. Moreover, the Saxon chronicler, Thomas Tartler, states: "There is one Vlach priest here in Şchei who, with no guidance, started cutting lead letters and printing, not in the usual manner but very shortly, glued them onto a wooden board and thus, printed a Vlach calendar with no printing press but with only a beam, and that is a highly time consuming and tiresome manner of doing printing"[32]. His calendar was actually widely spread both in Wallachia and in Moldova.

The books printed in the 17th century resemble much more books produced today than the printed materials of the 16th century. The similarities are:

- A title page (distinct from the cover), folio and, later, page numbering;
- A title page that is usually embellished;
- The printed material is richly decorated (displaying the country's emblem, as well);

31 Radu Tempea, op.cit., p. 132.

32 Apud, Octovian Şchiau (1968) *Cărturari şi cărţi în spaţiul românesc medieval* (Romanian for *Scholars and books in the within the Medieval Romanian Area*), Cluj-Napoca, 1978, p. 46.

- Book binding is done in special workshops. There are two ways of binding books: the one done in monasteries and consisting in leather wrapped wooden covers and the one characteristic of specialized workshops based on metal bindings.

Besides the above overview of the history of printed books in the Romanian language, an outline of the history of manuscripts that circulate at the same time with printed materials is mandatory.

First, it is worth remembering that for the time period covered by this book, the access to culture is still heavily constrained by social status. Thus, the Prince of Transylvania, Gabriel Bethlen establishes a college in Alba Iulia in 1622, whereas Vasile Lupu and Matei Basarab found higher education schools for the sons of rulers and rich people in Iaşi and Târgovişte in 1640. On the other hand, common people can barely read or write. Additionally, the price of books is pretty high and those who transcribe them on paper are monks, deacons, priests from the countryside or people who cherish their value. Last but not least, books are disseminated via different means, the manuscript representing one of these.

In the 17th century the number of manuscripts of a religious nature written in Slavonic or in Romanian diminishes (and as a result their price increases), while conversely, the number of secular manuscripts meant for reading and education increases. However, unlike the previous century, religious manuscripts are heavily sponsored by rulers and high representatives of the Orthodox Church. In light of this, it is worth noting the activity undertaken by Athanasie Crimca in Moldova, the founder of a school for copyists and miniaturists. Actually, the habit of engraving the portrait of the ruler, of his wife or the wealthy people of the country in manuscripts dates back to the 12th century. Some of the books widely circulated are: Varlaam şi Ioasaf (Varlaam and Ioasaf), Alexăndria[33], Esopia[34], as well as a new literary work by the name of 'cronografe' (popular history books that combine historical data with legends).

---

33 T.n. An almost homonymous title derived from the name of Alexander; the book is actually a famous novel in those times narrating the adventures of Alexander the Great.

34 An almost homonymous title derived from the name of Esop (Romanian for Aesop); the book includes the life and fables of Aesop.

The 17th century also records the publishing of the first official chronicles in the Romanian language usually dedicated to a specific ruler and serving obvious political goals. The activity of copying manuscripts becomes a lucrative one and is done by Chancery writers and secretaries. Some of the most significant names in this respect are: Fota, a Chancery secretary, who authors three copies of Varlaam and Ioasaf between 1671–1675; Ilie, a cantor from Iaşi, who transcribes books in Maramureş around 1697; Vasile Sturza Moldoveanul who copies 12 manuscripts from the villages around Orăştie, Arad and Timişoara; Toader, a Chancery writer in Braşov, who travels to Moldova in order to bring books and manuscripts; and last but not the least, Costea, a deacon in Şchei, Braşov. All of them are proof enough that the activity of the copyists from Moldova in Transylvania is unimpeded and there is an ongoing inflow and outflow of manuscripts between Wallachia, Moldova and Transylvania. Referring to that, Octavian Şchiau points out the following: "[the books] are translated in Wallachia or Moldova, copied and disseminated in Transylvania or they are translated in Transylvania and then copied in the other two countries, thus contributing to the spread of cultural values on both sides of the Carpathian mountains"[35], as well as "...the existence of a continuous spiritual contact among Romanians from everywhere is confirmed not only by the manifestation of the same spiritual and cultural preoccupations passed on until today, but also by the dedication shown by some modest scholars whose names old documents have barely recorded"[36].

Along with political alliances or commercial exchanges, such spiritual connections are but a part of the multiple relations developed among the three Romanian countries. However, it is worth mentioning that actually these forge the Romanian ethnic unity and consciousness. References to the above mentioned aspects, as well as to the similarities among the three Romanian provinces can be found in the chronicles of the time. For example, Ion Neculce's chronicle includes information and details concerning events from Wallachia; Radu Popescu, in turn, shows thorough knowledge of events from Moldova; and Radu Tempea refers to the people from across the mountains as 'brothers'.

---

35 Octavian Şchiau, op. cit, p. 64.
36 Ibidem, p. 30.

Transylvania "represents a source of information for the Romanian culture since, unlike other regions of the country, it best preserves hundreds and thousands of copies of books printed in the Romanian language and originating from all existing typographies"[37]. As such it actually represents a distilling retort for Romanian values.

The political situation in Transylvania in the 17th and 18th centuries prompts an attitude that values books and, hence, efforts to preserve and protect them. The most significant example from this point of view is the wide spread circulation of Varlaam's Cazania (Homilies) in all churches all around Transylvania, a book that is also known by the name of Carte românească de învăţătură (Romanian Book for Education). Apparently, the high demand for this book prompts the publishing of a second edition in 1643, the same year the first issue is released. According to Nicolae Iorga, there are 20 copies of the book in the churches around Braşov and Alba Iulia in 1905. Moreover, a researcher by the name of Bârlea discovers six copies in Maramureş, and six more are uncovered by Valeriu Literat in Wallachia. Nowadays, three copies of the book are in the Braşov County State Archives and one in the Museum of the the Church of Saint Nicholas in Şchei (a copy that comes from the parish of Stupina).

The Homilies of Metropolitan Varlaam proceed with a foreword by Vasile Lupu, the ruler of Moldova, addressed to: "all Romanians from everywhere who share the Orthodox faith and use the Romanian language"[38].

Another book of Varlaam, Predoslovie (an old Romanian word for Introduction), is addressed by the Metropolitan of Moldova to those who "...are Romanian, like us, and share the same faith wherever they are in Ardeal or in other countries[39]. The margin notes made in the copies of the above mentioned book show a wide circulation of the book, underpin the idea of Romanians' cultural unity and reveal the high esteem the owners had for it. For example, the copy consulted for this book that is in the County

---

37 Ibidem. p. 86.

38 APUD, Mircea Păcurariu, Hodoş dan, Simionescu (1903–1944) *Bibliografia românească veche*,(Romanian for *Old Romanian Bibliography)* vol. IV, Bucureşti, p. 170.

39 Ioan Bianu, Nerva Hodoş, Dan Simionescu (1903–1944) *Bibliografia românească veche*,(Romanian for *Old Romanian Bibliography)*, vol. IV, Bucureşti, p. 170.

State Archives of Braşov has a variegated history: in 1686 it is in Voşlobani-Mureş, a century later, in 1792 it is sold to the priest Elisei from Daia by his cousin, Mojan Popa Lascu, and ten years later Onea Bordea along with his family purchase it and donate it to the church in Daia. The information on the margin notes of the copy in Şchei is provided in the appendices.

Simion Ştefan, Metropolitan of Transylvania, emphasizes in clear-cut terms the same idea of ethnic unity in his preface to the New Testament, issued in Bălgrad, in 1648: "However, here it is what you need to heed : Romanians from other countries do not use the same vocabulary to talk about their outfit or about many other things. Therefore, they may need someone to write in such a manner that they can all understand what is written. It is common knowledge that words must be like money: it is only money that circulates all over the world that it is worth something, and similarly with the words that can be understood by everybody"[40]. One particular work that is worth recalling is Chiriacodromion, printed in Bălgrad, in 1699 by the typographer Mihail Istvanovici. The latter is sent to Transylvania by Brâncoveanu so that, under the guidance of Athanasie Anghel, Metropolitan of Ardeal, and based on a text edited, with minor changes, in Moldova, a new edition of Varlaam's Cazania (Homilies) intended for the readers in Transylvania is re-published. Other widely distributed books are: Evanghelia (The Gospel) printed in Bucharest in 1682 and Apostolul (The Apostles- a book used in the Orthodox church and including events from the lives of the Apostles, as well as their epistles) printed in Bucharest a year later.

The Bible, published in Bucharest in 1688 and translated by the brothers from Şerban Greceanu's family, was distributed in a limited edition. Thus, it can be found only in the most important cultural centers of Transylvania because "Given its extremely high price, people from small villages could not afford to purchase it because of their financial constraints"[41].

In conclusion, all of the above contribute to providing an overview of old Romanian books, either in printed form or as manuscripts mostly during the 17th century.

---

40 Octavian Şchiau, op. cit. p. 90.

41 Vasile Oltean (1989) *Şcoala românească din Şcheii Braşovului*,(Romanian for *The First School in Romanian Language from Şchei, Braşov*) Bucureşti, p. 55.

3.2 Margin notes in 17th century old Romanian books in Şchei, Braşov

Before focusing on the topic of this sub-chapter, some important observations need to be made. On one hand, the time frame for some margin notes made in books or manuscripts is the 17th century, when these were actually published. On the other hand, there are older margin notes that, because of their importance, were copied in publications that were issued much later. Last but not the least, there are also notes made later than the 17th century by book readers or owners.

The research on margin notes is concerned with the way they emerged and how they are perceived nowadays. In this respect, these notes are almost a literary genre of its own for the age when they were made and their tradition continues until the 19th century when they are replaced by diaries with daily entries.

The phenomenon of margin notes made in books emerges when the number of events in the external environment increases to the extent that the trust in the possibility of conveying messages orally vanishes. Thus, scholars, cantors, priests, copyists become aware of the power of the written message to make them eternal. A person's memory may, more often than not, play tricks on him/her, whereas what is written is permanent. Additionally, there is also the respect of the medieval person for what is written. All of the above may account for the diminishing number of notes in the 19th century when the printed book and even the manuscript is no longer a novelty.

In the margin notes dating back to the 17th century which are the object of our scientific investigation, there are few personal events worth recording in writing, whereas there are many references to the Romanian community in Şchei that provide valuable information. Most of those who write margin notes either work with the church or school in Şchei, or are learned people. All of them value books as a means to enlighten the human soul. From this perspective, people who can read and write are able to view the world differently, with their mind's eye. Because of the special position of books, nothing ordinary could go in margin notes.

Nonetheless, the situation changes in the 18th century when the number of margin notes increases. They are made by common people who feel tempted to record minor personal events. However, even these notes represent the way these persons think.

Most of the notes are made in a specific pattern that is not altered. Books are valuable items meant to circulate and therefore one cannot write just anything in the notes. Moreover, since for the medieval person keeping time was not standardized like today, many of the notes are not dated. In this respect, for the 17th century it is more important to record an event related to politics, meteorology, community, rather than the exact date when it occurs. Time was kept in those times by referring to Easter and Christmas, the most important religious holidays. Therefore, the information in some notes can only be used with reservations since approaching them from a historical perspective requires knowledge of their time frame. As for the relation between the texts of the books and the notes made on their margins, there are texts that summarize and comment on the content of the books (most often such comments are quotes from the Bible or the Psalms as normative and moral references). Nevertheless, most of the notes have no relation whatsoever with book content.

Concerning the relationship between notes and historical events, there are notes meant to prevent information from fading away and notes made by a literary pattern and which include common references to earlier writings. The notes in the 17th century are a literary genre, playing the role of chronicles. As such, compared to the chronicles of ruling officials, the notes raise a distance between the writer and the reader.

Margin notes disappear when this type of chronicle becomes a daily recording of events and with the emergence of travel diaries. Nowadays, margin notes are only preserved by the personal comments made on the texts we read.

The analysis of the margin notes made in the 17th century manuscripts and printed books in Şchei, Braşov, is to focus on the following topics:

- Attitudes towards books;
- Information on book distribution and the cultural relationships unveiled by this;
- The school of copyists in Şchei;
- Reproductions of older notes that contribute to the dating effort;
- Historical events as presented by notes;

- Events from the city as portrayed by notes;
- Weather phenomena as described by the notes.

A. Attitudes towards books

The focus of this investigation are books, either in printed form or in manuscript, as they were distributed from Wallachia and Moldova to Ardeal, or copied all around Transylvania, and that reached Şchei, as well as the books copied in accordance with the tradition of the school that functioned in Şchei, Braşov. Generally speaking, margin notes reflect the attitude of the copyist or of the reader towards the book itself or related to the environment. Personal feelings are rather difficult to spot in these notes, but there are some instances of more personalized approaches. The handwritten text provides information that allows the identification of the persons who made the note, as well as additional details on their identity. Starting from the perspective presented in the notes, critical assessments of events and data are possible. The focus of this research is not only on books meant for the common use, but also as part of commercial transactions.

a. Books as items of value and of common use

Before exemplifying the instances in which books are viewed as items of value, as well as articles of common use, we first need to analyze the attitude of the people who had access to books, as well as their roles and positions. Those who write margin notes in books are copyists of manuscripts who record their name or their position, owners, buyers, inheritors or simply people who had the chance to hold the books in their hands. Readers' notes, especially of those who learn how to write and read based on religious books, usually record their skill development. There are also notes of those who ordered the book and paid for it entirely or partially, of donors –in this case, the notes include, besides the person's name, chronological information and book price, or notes that place a curse on whoever may dare to steal the book. Last but not least, buyers' notes underline book price.

Copyists' attitudes towards books reflect the efforts made to transcribe them, as well as their awareness of the importance of leaving written pieces for generations to come. It is common knowledge that most books were used for didactical purposes. Some notes help identify the copyist and the date when the book was transcribed (document 1 in appendices). For example, in one such note in a book entitled Parâmierul *românesc* (*Romanian Chant Book for Lent*), there is a handwritten reference to a protopope and chronicler, Vasile: “Vasile wrote the book when he served as a cantor and Chancery secretary, before becoming a protopope”[42].

In some notes, the name of the copyist is mentioned but with no further personal details (appendices, document no. 4): priest Oprea serving in the church in Şchei, Ioan Pisăriul (a copyist), Vâlcu, a Chancery secretary. In terms of donors’ notes, document 3 provides the following information: the book is purchased by Iuga Pojar, boyard of Wallachia and donated to the church in Şchei in 1611. Additionally, in document no. 2 Barbu Hoban, makes a note that identifies him as a cantor who filled this position after 1680, and as the son of Vasile Hoban II. Similarly, in document no. 5, the notes record the names and positions of people: *Micul* (Mihul) acting as cantor in Şchei in 1697, and Matei, son of priest Oprea, a former priest in Satulung.

All of the above, along with the information provided by the records of the church in Şchei that list the names of the priests and cantors having served, as well as their commitments made upon joining the school and their salaries, offer a general outlook that is a proof of cultural continuity.

A special type of note refers to the book itself, as it is the case of Vasile Hoban, the son of protopope Văsii Hoban presented in document 14 dated 1680. However, this category will be handled in a separate chapter.

There are notes that trace the path followed by books, as in document no. 3 which refers to a book known as Minei de februarie (The February Menaion). This was donated in 1611 and the first entry referring to the use of the book in Şchei is dated March 1st, 1652 and is written by the Chancery secretary,Vâlcu. The scribble on its covers proves that the book was frequently used for didactic purposes.

The notes also offer information on the owner who can be either a private person or an institution, namely the church: either the church in Şchei

42 Ibidem, p. 69.

or those from nearby Brașov. Examples of such texts are in documents no. 4 and 11, while the note in document 24 a. refers to a book owned by the church from Cincu Mare in 1881. However, there are also mentions of books donated by various people to the church or to the school in Șchei.

Donations were part of charity work. However, the concept of charity in those times does not mean the same thing as nowadays. Consequently, these donations were actually meant to enrich the heritage of the school or of the church as items to be used for religious or for educational purposes. Some names of donors provided by the notes in document 25 a are: Johann Georg Christiani, most likely a well-known person from within the town council; Bartolomeu Baiulescu, protopope of Brașov; Radu Boghici who, in 1783, was a member of a family of merchants by the same name in Șchei. The notes in documents 4 and 10 record as a donor one of the high profile people of the church, that is Ghenadie, Metropolitan of Ardeal. The documents bearing the latter's handwriting are printed in Russia, but there is no information as to how they reached him. What is clearly specified, though, is that document no. 10 by the name of Cuvântare apostolească (Apostle's Homily) is his donation to the church in Șchei.

The notes often include curses that are supposed to act as restraints on book theft. As such, they are closely related to people's attitude towards books. At the time, when Christian values were highly viewed and common people feared Divinity, they were the only means of prevention against book theft. In this respect, the Apostles and the 318 Holy Fathers Assembled in the City of Nice are often invoked by these curses. Some of the sentences used are as follows: "...and nobody shall dare to take it from where I placed it, and whoever shall will to take it, that shall never be forgiven by God, all saints or me, the sinner, nor will he ever be released from this curse, Amen" (see document no. 2); "...and whoever may be tempted to steal it shall be anathema" (see document no. 25 a). One of the most impressive curses is the one from document no. 21: "...and whoever may strive to steal it from my hands or from my children's hands, may the devil steal his soul and take it in the same place where Judas' is".

These curses were meant to be book guardians. Books were not only personal property, but they were also goods of the community. In such cases, the curses also mention that the book could be alienated only with the agreement of church synod (see document no. 10).

The notes also provide information on where a book is at a given moment in time. For example, in Evanghelie (Romanian for Gospel), printed in Govora, in 1642, these notes place the book in Târgovişte until 1753, and two decades later, in 1773 the book can be found in Şchei, Braşov. (see document no. 11).

b. Books as commodities

People's attitudes towards books are also reflected by how they treat them as commodities. Their value is expressed in money. However, to understand their real value one should first understand the value of land –which is the safest commodity at the time. To finance a book could be very expensive since it involves various operations that have to be paid: book translation, copying and binding. As a result, most often books are purchased collectively and afterwards donated to the church. For example, document no. 21 mentions the sale of a book for 15 German coins, a price equivalent to that of a plot of land, whereas the notes in document no. 12 made in a book from Feldioara mention its purchase for 22.8 zlotys gained from selling a piece of land. Another copy of the same book is bought for 10 zlotys by a priest from Calbor, in 1805. Some of the notes indicate that the value of books, expressed as a fixed amount of money, is pretty high when compared with the value of estate or land. In this respect, the price of books determines their purchase in pieces. The owner only binds the book after having purchased all parts it (even binding books is a costly operation). There are notes that mention the binding of book parts in Şchei, like the Tipicul grecesc (The Greek Ritual) (document no. 19), a book in Greek that is "a proof of education level and of the fact that this language was used in the school in Şchei"[43].

The activity of rebinding books as a result of the inherent wear and tear involved by didactical activities is also recorded by the margin notes. That is not only a sign of respect for cultural values, but it also involves a lot of pride (see document 27). For example, in Mineiul pe februarie (The February Menaion) there is a note by Radu Tempea II, dated 1727 that records his efforts to bind the book for the second time.

---

43 Constantin Lacea *Biblioteca veche a bisericii Sfântul Nicolae din Braşov* (Romanian for The Old Library of Saint Nicholas Church from Braşov), in "Transilvania", no. 1, Jan-March 1909, p. 100–106.

The sale deed for a book is drawn up in the presence of witnesses. For example, in document no. 21 there are at least four people witnessing the book sale and they write their names in the book margins.

Alms are one way of using books as commodity. In this respect, it involves ordering the book or buying it and, afterwards, offering it for the souls of the departed with a view to having them cleansed of their sins (see document no. 12, copy VI). In this respect, according to the Orthodox faith, good deeds grant the cleansing of sin.

3.3 Information on book distribution. Book binding

The margin notes also tell about the cultural centers of the time, as well their inter-connections. The material perused for this scientific investigation allows tracing the path of books up until the 19th century: starting from the printing/copying stage, all throughout intermediary stages like purchase, donations or alms. In this respect, the available information indicates the important role played by Brașov as a result of its geographical position. The town is well known for its permanent contact with the areas in the South and East of Carpathians, as well as for being at the crossroads of the Balkan Peninsula and Western countries. All of the above is mentioned in the books printed in the West that are archived in Șchei.

a. Books from Wallachia

A number of printed materials date back to the times of Matei Basarab.

Evanghelie învățătoare (Gospel for Instruction) is printed in Târgoviște in 1650 (document no. 14) and bears an undated margin note made by Mircaș, a *logofăt*[44] (the very name of the position used by this person as a means of identification shows that the book can be placed in Wallachia since no such position existed in Transylvania at the time).

Îndreptarea legii (Law Anthology) is printed in Tărgoviște (document no. 15), and several printed copies of this are in the Șchei archive. One of them is recorded as the collective property belonging to the church from

44 A position characteristic for Middle Ages Wallachia and Moldova that referred to a high dignitary from within the hierarchy of boyards that also involved acting as a councilor to the ruler.

the village of Mătereuş. Another one is part of the heritage of the Bărans, a family of priests. It bears a margin note mentioning the year 1736. Another sample comes from Sâmbăta monastery, nearby Făgăraş, and is bought in 1738 by protopope Şerban. Various printed copies or manuscripts of the same document reach the villages nearby Braşov and from here the Şchei archive. That is evidence again that the school and church in Şchei make this neighborhood an important cultural center within the Bârsa Country, as well as the axis of relationships established across a wide geographical area.

Şerban Cantacuzino is another Wallachian ruler who takes the initiative to print books in the Romanian language. Upon his order, a book titled Apostol (Apostle's Homily) is printed in Bucharest, in 1683. As mentioned by a brief margin note made by the cantor serving in the church from Făgăraş, one of its copies can be traced in the above mentioned place in 1799. Later on, the book is brought from Grânar to Şchei, according to the records of the church from this neighborhood.

Another book printed under the authority of the same ruler is Evanghelia elinească şi rumânească (The Gospel in Greek and Romanian – document no. 22) printed in Bucharest in 1693. This book is traced back to the church of Păpăuţiului (a village near Târgu Secuiesc) in1790, and later offered as alms to the church from Lisnău from where, most likely, it reaches Şchei.

The Şchei archive owns several copies of Evanghelia (The Gospel), printed in Snagov (document no. 23). In 1699, one of these copies can be traced back to the church from Bundead (Boiu nearby Sighişoara). A manuscript of this book is financed by the Boghici's, a family in Şchei referred to in a margin note by Oprea Boghici dated 1722.

Last but not least, another book printed under Şerban Cantacuzino is Biblia de la Bucureşti (Romanian for The Bucharest Bible). One of its copies, exquisitely printed, that bears no margin notes, is exhibited in the museum of the First School in Romanian Language in Şchei.

Many valuable books issued under Constantin Brâncoveanu, a ruler well-known for the relationships established with the people from Braşov, reached the cultural center of Şchei and can be found in church inventory. Since most of them date back to the 18th century, they are not part of the analysis undertaken in this book. However, they are worth mentioning:

Mineiul pe luna septembrie (The September Menaion) (document no. 24 b); Minei pe luna ianuarie (The January Menaion) (document no. 26) bearing a margin note made by Radu Tempea II in 1727; Minei pe luna februarie (The February Menaion) (document no. 27); Minei pe luna martie şi aprilie (The March and April Menaion) (document no. 28) printed in Buzău in1689, a copy of which is distributed in Huşi, Moldova, which then becomes the property of the Romanian Church United with Rome (Greek Catholic church) from Făgăraş in 1843 (according to the margin note written by the cantor Adam Caţavei). From this point of view, it is worth underlining that the Greek Catholic church from Făgăraş maintains its relationship with the Orthodox Church in Şchei and uses a religious book issued under Orthodox sponsorship.

In conclusion, the books from Wallachia are donated by both this country's rulers and by the boyars. For example, Mineiul pe februarie (The February Menaion) (document no. 3), as well as Tipicul grecesc (The Greek Ritual) (document no. 20) are donated by Iuga Pojar, a boyar. Concerning Tipicul grecesc, this is bought by a monk from Câmpina who then is allowed by the synod to sell it to the church in Şchei.

b. Books from Moldova

Even though, as a result of geographical factors, the relationships between Braşov and Wallachia are numerous and illustrative for the 17th century, the ones between Braşov and Moldova are equally obvious. Thus, the book entitled Carte românească de învăţătură (Romanian Book for Education) (document no. 12) issued during the rule of Vasile Lupul, reaches Şchei in several copies through Feldioara, Calbor and Hârseni. One of these copies is recorded in the church inventory of Şchei as "a religious document from Varlaam of Moldova"[45]. Additionally, one can find in Şchei a *Minei salvon pe luna ianuarie* (A Slavonic January Menaion) (document no. 6) that comes from Putna monastery, and a Tipic slavon (Slavonic Ritual) (document no. 9), donation on behalf of Moldova's treasurer, Teodor Boul, and

45 Vasile Oltean, *Descoperirea unui codice-miscelaneum în limba română,(Romanian for The Dicovery of a Miscellaneum Codex in the Romanian Language)* in "România literară", no. 5, 1975, p. 19.

his wife, Agahia, to the church in Şchei, dated 1610 and that can still be found in the archives of this religious institution.

c. Books from Transylvania

An important center for printing materials in Transylvania is Alba Iulia (Bălgarad), and an important role in this respect is played by the rulers of this region. Some of these books that can be found in the archive in Şchei are as follows: one copy of Noul Testament (The New Testament) edited upon the order of Gheorghe Rakoczy I, one copy of Evanghelie învăţătoare (Gospel for Instruction) (of which there are actually several copies in Braşov) (document no. 24 a) issued under Gheorghe Banfy (1685–1689), governor of Transylvania during the reign of Joseph II and Cuvântarea apostolească (The Apostle's Homily) (document no. 10), a copy of which is a donation on behalf of Ghenadie, Metropolitan of Ardeal (1627–1640), to the church in Şchei.

d. Books from Russia

The presence of works printed in Ukraine in Braşov is the result of the cultural relations established by priests and cantors in Şchei, Braşov with Ukraine and Russia while travelling to Moscow. Moreover, this can also be attributed to the role played by Petru Movilă, Metropolitan of Kiev and patron of the school from the Pacerskaia monastery, an important center of the Orthodox faith. Some of the books printed in Russia that are nowadays in Şchei are: Tipic slavon (Slavonic Ritual) (document no. 6), Istoria lui Varlaam şi Ioasaf (The History of Varlaam and Ioasaf (inventory no. 93), Minei slavon pe luna mai (A Slavonic May Menaion) (inventory no. 32), Tâlc de evanghelie (Gospel's Interpretation), Apostol cu cuvântări (Apostle's Homilies), Disputa creştinilor cu jidovii despre Mesia (Christian's and Jews'Dispute on Mesiah) (document no. 18).

e. Books from other cultural centers

The books that are currently in the archives of Şchei come from a variety of places. Germany ranks first with its printing centers in Nuremberg, Heidelberg (Unterschliedlicher Gotesdienste in der ganzer Welt- inventory no. 1026), Frankfurt am Main (Noul Testament: The New Testament, inventory no. 1465), Wittenberg (Martin Luther, Biblie: Bible, inventory no. 1170), Leipzig (Saint Macarius, Omilii: Homilies, inventory no. 974). The books from Poland come from Danzig (Iohanne Latermano, Ceaneae theologorm ortodoxum, inventory no. 760). Other books come from Athens: one copy (document no. 20), Italy: one book in Greek and Latin printed in Venice in 1642, Expositu patrum grecorum im psalmos, inventory no. 1303, Corpus Bizantinae historiae, inventory no. 1327), Geneva in Switzerland: Francois Turretin, Requel de sermos sne divers textes de L'ecritures S. Pour l' etat de l'eglise, inventory no. 1032.

All of the above, however, bear no margin notes and, hence, are not the object of our analysis.

3.4 Margin notes on the school of copyists in Șchei

a. Manuscripts copied in Şchei in the 17th century

The school of copyists in Şchei brings an important contribution to Romanian culture that is treated both in **Chapter II: ŞCHEI, BRAŞOV – A CULTURAL CENTER OF ROMANIANS**, and in **Annexes**.

One important book among those consulted for this study is Parâmierul românesc, (*Romanian Chant Book for Lent*), a manuscript transcribed by Vasile, the chronicler, in 1613, which is "a codex in the Romanian language dating back to the end of the 16th century, authored by four scholars of Şchei, well known for their cultural and scholarly activities within the school of copyists in Şchei and in Wallachia"[46]. The book consists of four parts written by different authors. The largest one is authored by Vasile, the chronicler: "the first part is attributed to Vasile Hoban, identified by the above name, and to his son, Ioan, a Chancery secretary; the second part is written by priest Vasile's brother, protopope Constantin (1576–1629), a scholar concerned with procuring books and donating them, according to other margin notes; the fourth part is authored by Văsii Hoban (the nephew of the first copyist already mentioned) and describes the battle of Zărneşti dated 1690"[47].

46 Ibidem, p. 19.
47 Vasile Oltean, The First School in the Romanian Language, pp. 91–94.

Judging by the way the manuscript looks today, it is obvious that it was intensely used in school, since its authors acted as cantors and priests in the church in Şchei and they arranged the information by topics. In this respect, "the manuscript transcribed by the school of copyists in Şchei that was used by Coresi may have disappeared along with a box filled with books and documents, as David Corbea notes in the oldest record of the church dated 1684"[48]. Thus, it is obvious that many other sources that could have contributed useful information to our scientific study are unavailable.

Another document used for the purposes of this book is Minei slavon pe lunile martie şi aprilie (Slavonic March and April Menaion) (document no. 4). This manuscript is the work of several local copyists, according to the margin notes written on its covers. It mentions names like: Vasilache, Teodor, Vâlcu, people known for their intense activity in the school in Şchei. According to a note dated 1611, the manuscript is the property of the church in Şchei and, like many other, comes from the collection of protopope Mihai.

Additionally, the study relies on an illustrated Manual de filosofie (Philosophy Handbook) (document no. 2) that is part of church archive. This is composed of several parts bound together and it is actually a collection of concepts related to ethics and moral behavior written by Barbu Hoban. Moreover, it includes "excerpts from Învăţăturile duhovniceşti [Spiritual Precepts] by Petru Damaschin and from the work of Simion Metafrasul, a hagiographer from the 10th century"[49], along with fragments from the work of Socrates, Demosthenes, Aristotle, Zeno. "The second part of this manuscript comes from another manuscript copied at the beginning of the 16th century by Barbu Hoban, whereas its last part includes five pages copied by the same person which replicate homiletic comments on Credeiu (The Creed)"[50]. The manuscript bears the signatures of various cantors

48 Ibidem, pp. 97–98.

49 Vasile Oltean, *Semnificaţia documentului voievodal de la 1665 descoperit în Şcheii Braşovului,* (Romanian for *The Significance of the Voivode's Deed of 1665 discovered in Şchei, Braşov*) in "Astra", 1985, no. 7, pp. 10–11.

50 Apud, Gabriel Ştrempel, *Manuscrisele româneşti aflate la Leningrad şi Kiev,* (Romanian for *The Romanian Manuscripts from Leningrad and Kiev*) in "Studii şi cercetări de bibliografie"(Romanian for Bibliographical *Studies and Researches*), 1972, XII, p. 25.

and copyists in Şchei: Oprea, the Chancery secretary, Stanciu and Barbu Hoban.

A rather large publication is recorded in the archives of the church under the title of *Pomelnicul mare* (The Extended List of the Living and the Deceased – document no. 16) organized by two columns. One includes the list of rulers and their wives who sponsored the church in Şchei, which begins with Neagoe Basarab and continues up to Eustatie Dabija and his wife, Dafina. In the other column, there is a list including the names of cantors and priests who served the church for a time, local merchants who had ties with the church, as well as boyars from Moldova and Wallachia. The author of this list is the same as the one of the Philosophy Handbook.

The work entitled Epistolie (Epistle), attributed to a member of the Hoban's, Văsii Hoban is an ample one including a lot of apophthegmatic information from Molitvelnic (The Book of Common Prayer) or Sinaxar (Synaxarion), as well as personal information concerning its author (document no. 21) and dates of funerals.

In the margin notes of Minei slavon pe luna august (Slavonic August Menaion) (document no. 17) cantor Pătru, son of merchant Gheorghe Făinăbună in Şchei, takes credit for writing the book.

All of the above manuscripts belonging to the school of copyists in Şchei are important historical sources. However, there must have been many more that either disappeared or cannot be identified because of poor preservation.

b. Dissemination of Şchei manuscripts

Gabriel Ştrempel makes an important contribution to the analysis of manuscripts in the Romanian language that are in libraries from Leningrad sau Kiev. His study emphasizes the existence of a work entitled Liturghier slavo-român (Liturgical Prayer in Slavo-Romanian) dated 1662. As proof that the manuscript was the property of the Church of Saint Nicholas, there are two seals on its cover belonging to the above mentioned church in Şchei. The margin notes in the manuscript are as follows:

Folio 200: "Let it be known that the beginning of this Liturgical Prayer /sic/ belonging to priest Vasilache from Braşov is written by Vasiliova Ghelasie, a monk from the monastery /sic/ of Dobromirna, who then died. Afterwards, I, Ioan, a Chancery writer, born in Ardeal, from the region Cetatea de Baltă that is located on the Târnava Mică river (*The Small Târnava River*), from the Carchiel cel Mare village (*The Big Carchiel* village), son of Arâmboc Andonie, strove to write the Zlătăust (old Romanian for *Prayer* of Saint *John Chrysostom*) and the Peulejştena used during fasting periods, as well as the Acatist (title of prayer to the Virgin Mary or to saints), I finished my endeavor in Moldova, at Bistriţa monastery during the rule of Istratie Dabija, the voivode. At the time of finishing this writing, 7170 (1662), April 18, Apafz Mihaiu was the ruler of Ţara Ungurească (literally the Hungarian country in Romanian) when there were Turks and Tatars burning and enslaving the country"[51].

The text above highlights that the first part of the manuscript belongs to Ghelasie, a former monk from Soveja, and that the one who worked to finish it was a chancery secretary by the name of Ion (Ioan?) from Cetatea de Baltă. The latter finalized the manuscript in Moldova at Bistriţa monastery.

What is worth noticing is that the manuscript has margin notes. One of these is written by protopope Văsii in Şchei, who offers the book to the church as alms:

"I, Văsii in Şchei have given this blessed Liturgical Prayer to the holy church to use it until the end of time. And I offered this book as alms for my wife, Neacşa. And whoever may be tempted to sell it or estrange it or delete these words that shall be excommunicated, anathema and banished by Lord Christ 300 and 18 times; dated 7172–1664".

Referring to the above note, Ştrempel underlined the following:

"there was no one to delete the inscription of protopope Vasile; however, there was someone with no fear of the curse and who, travelling pretty often to Russia took the manuscript and gave it to some high ecclesiastic figure from this Orthodox country"[52].

51 Ibidem, p. 27.

52 Apud, Valeria Leu, *Circulaţia cărţii româneşti în valea Almăjului până la 1840, (Circulation of Romanian Books on Almăjului Valley until 1840)* in "Banatica", The History Museum of Caraş- Severin county, Reşiţa, 1979, pp. 477–483.

An unusual manuscript discovered by the researcher Leu Valeria in the Precista church from Galaţi, belongs to Radu Tempea II. This manuscript is the transcript of Tâlcul liturghiei (Liturgy's Interpretation) (printed in Iaşi during Antioh Cantemir) and includes a margin note on the attack of the Turks in Cameniţa in 1700, as well as a note written by Radu Tempea in Latin on folio 265: "Cum dai mizericordia legistusum et Schripei hoc Librum et ego Radu Ierey Tempe. Corona, Anno 1724. die Graţios ego ami nihi dedit"[53].

c. Manuscripts from around Braşov that reached Şchei

The list of residences provided in the appendices is a very good starting point for tracing the path of manuscripts around Braşov and in the region before reaching Şchei. In this respect, there are two such significant examples. The first is Cartea româneascaă de învăţătură (The Romanian Book for Education) (document no. 12) that reaches Şchei from the church in Feldioara, and Apostolul (The Apostle's Homily) (document no. 19), that belonged to the church from Făgăraş.

As for manuscripts copied outside Şchei which only afterwards reached this cultural neighborhood, unfortunately there is only one such example: one copy of Evanghelie (The Gospel) (document no. 23 copy no. II) copied by Pop Dumitru from Târlungeni.

3.5 Reproductions of older margin notes supporting dating

It is worth recalling that margin notes from the 17th century rarely record personal feeling. However, what is characteristic of the people who make them is that they love writing and, hence, their margin notes may be copies of older notes that they found important to record, even without accurate dating of the events. This carelessness about dating events can be explained from the perspective of collective mentality: an event was viewed as important depending on the nature of the information related to it and its impact upon people's mentality and not as part of a chronological order of dates. One such example are the margin notes in Apostol

53 Apud, Vasile Oltean, *Cronici şi cronicari la Şcheii Braşovului* (Romanian for *Chronicles and chroniclers in Şchei, Braşov)* in "Astra", 1973, no. 2, p. 14.

cu cuvântări (Apostle Homilies and Allocutions) (document no. 13), a book printed in Moscow in 1643, that records how Preda Buzescu, one of the captains of Michael the Brave, is brought wounded to Braşov. Moreover, they also report about the unsuccessful attempts of the local doctors to treat him.

Thus, dating events as accurately as possible based on the information conveyed by margin notes is rather difficult.

3.6 Political events as presented by margin notes

The information provided by margin notes on historical events is scarce in the 17th century, whereas they abound in the 18th century. The most common references of a historical nature concern the rulers who cherished their connections with Braşov and viewed this town as a refuge.

Thus, in Parâmierul românesc (*Romanian Chant Book for Lent*) (document no. 1), there is a note made by Vasile Hoban II, a witness to the battle from Zărneşti between the Turks and the Austrians which unfolded in 1690, that highlights the fact that even though Constantin Brâncoveanu was present in the area, he did not participate in the event.

It is common knowledge that both the school and the church in Şchei benefitted from many donations over the years. In this respect, the trips made by the priests from Şchei were viewed as important events by the community and hence recorded in the margin notes. For example, in 1731, the priest Teodor Băran journeys to the ruler of Moldova, Grigore Ghica, in order to obtain a donation deed (document no. 27).

The notes also record the frequent invasions of the Austrians in Transylvania (document no. 24 copy no. 4).

There are also notes from the late 17th century that are copied simply because they were already in the 17th century books, as it is the case with those referring to the events of 1848 (document no. 15, copy no. II).

Some notes also provide comparisons between two Wallachian rulers: Brâncoveanu and Şerban Cantacuzino. While the former's administration is described as one of joy for the people since "the poor, the rich and the merchants had no idea what exile meant" and the ruler was like "the bee that heaps up its wealth", Cantacuzino is characterized as a person who "digs up a hole, scoops it up and falls into the pit he has made". Another note on Mavrocordat states the following: "whenever God wants to punish a country it does so by appointing an evil ruler"[54].

3.7 Local events as reflected by annotations

The local events are the most beautiful and interesting ones recorded by margin notes. They refer to community and to unusual phenomena and as such they actually describe the mentality of the age and a certain manner of perceiving things. These types of events are minutely reported as it is the case of a tower's collapse (document no. 13), that seems to be an example of how older notes are replicated.

Another important local event recorded by the notes made by Teodor Băran (document no. 27) is the donation granted by Brâncoveanu. This makes the following statement concerning the merchants from Şchei: "they come from an old family of boyars", a sentence that highlights the fact that the nobility in Şchei had old origins.

The families of merchants from Şchei supported the school and the church which was part of a tradition that is recorded by local history. Thus, unlike Wallachia, this history is also recorded in the margin notes. For example, the community in Şchei would gather on the church portico anytime there were important, more or less sad events, like funerals, as reported by document no. 21. Such events allow for the information in books to be disseminated and the priests and cantors, who could read and write, played a major role in this respect both in school and in church.

One happy event is recorded by document no. 25 b. It refers to the christening of three twins in the church in Şchei.

The notes also record family events (marriages, births, Christening, burials) and community related experiences (document no. 2). An example of a community event is the oath made by Radu Murgan to stop drinking and to show respect for his wife and household. Breaking the oath entails a severe punishment in front of the whole community. The note referring to this is made by Vasile Hoban and it portrays perfectly the Romanian community, its customs and severe laws. The fact that such an oath is

54 Ibidem, p. 19.

written in the margin note in a book is more evidence of how much the people valued this medium.

The margin notes also help identify names of people and families (document no. 18) by presenting for example the members of the Marcea or Boghici family (document no. 23), the merchant family by the name of *Cătană* (document no. 29), the Tempea family (document no. 25 and 26) or by presenting lists of the deceased. In one of the notes from document no. 17, there is the name of a well-known merchant from Braşov: *Gheorghe Făinăbună*[55], a typical case of using somebody's nickname as a last name. This person is also mentioned as a witness to the deeds signed by Brâncoveanu with the merchants from Şchei.

The notes also provide information on commercial transactions (document no. 2) and their recording is a sign that they are worth remembering.

In conclusion, margin notes also play an important role in describing in a detailed manner the local events experienced by the community of Romanians living in Şchei.

3.8 Meteorological phenomena as illustrated by margin notes

Last but not the least, the margin notes refer to unusual meteorological phenomena like a devastating hail in the Târgovişte area (document no. 11) in 1772, the early winter in October 1775 (document no. 21) that affected both humans and animals, or a very long winter that lasted until Easter time (document no. 13).

To sum up, this chapter offered an organization of the information presented by the margin notes made in the old Romanian books consulted for this study by domains. However, before moving on to the next chapter and discussing the place of Şchei in the history of the 17th century, it is important to discuss the nature of the 17th century books from the inventory of the church from the above mentioned neighborhood of Braşov.

First of all, most of the books are of a religious nature and were used both in church and as educational material in school. Apart from

55 T.n. the literal translation of *Făinăbună* is "good flour" but metaphorically it actually refers to the high quality of the person nicknamed as such.

Evanghelia (The Gospel) that includes not only the story of Jesus Christ, but also parts of the Old Testament, there are also Cazania (Homilies) which explain the text of The Gospel, collections of sermons included in Omilii (Homilies) and Liturghiere (Liturgical Books) that refer to events of a religious nature, a large collection on Minee (Menaions), namely a type of calendar issued for one or several months and that contain references to the holy days and stories of a moral-religious nature, and last but not least a collection of Psalmi (Psalms) in Greek, that shows that this language was studied in the school in Şchei.

The second category of books consists of books like Îndreptarea legii (Law Anthology) and Carte românească de învăţătură (Romanian Book for Education) of which there are two copies in the Şchei inventory.

The number of secular books is smaller by comparison. Some of the most important ones are: O istorie a Bizanţului (A History of Byzantium) in Latin, Herodotus' Istorii (Histories) and a Cronică a Ungariei (A Chronicle of Hungary).

All of the above simply highlight that the 17th century Romanian community in Şchei, Braşov, was an important one that had a demand for books in the Romanian language and used them for religious and educational purposes. Moreover, it is obvious that the town of Braşov was in contact with the cultural centers from across the Carpathians, as well as to other European cultural centers.

Chapter IV. Şchei, Braşov –At the Crossroads of Romanian aspirations

MOTTO "*For a peaceful and satisfying (religious) conversion the covertly and yet powerfully throbbing blood and spiritual bonds among the Romanians from Wallachia, Moldova and Transylvania should be first broken. By no means the rulers of the above mentioned countries are to allow that and will definitely intercept any attempts in this respect, if not with arms, then with covert advice.*"

(the reply of Constantinople's patriarch, Kiril Lucaris, to the letter of Prince Bethlen proposing the conversion of the Romanians from Ardeal to Calvinism-September 2, 1629).

The quote above is significant for the close ties of language and nationality of Romanians expressed by the Orthodox religion, which has never been suppressed regardless of the pressures to which its adherents have been subjected. Without the ongoing support of the rulers and high ranking priests from Wallachia and Moldova, this faith could not have survived.

Şchei, the Romanian neighborhood of Braşov is a relevant example of this. It is the place where spiritual activities emerge as a result of the relationships established between Braşov and other Romanian territories. Officially, these relationships are grounded in the political and commercial interests of the Saxons from Braşov.

Due to its geographical positioning, Braşov has always been closer to Wallachia than to the capital city of Transylvania. It has always been on the border of the two countries and consequently, whenever the political situation in Wallachia became uncertain, the town was used as a refuge for the oppressed. For the time period covered by the scientific investigation undertaken in this book, Transylvania was deeply influenced by the Union created by Michael the Brave, as well as by the rule of several Calvinist princes who pushed for the conversion of the Romanian population from Transylvania to Calvinism. Under these circumstances, the Orthodox Church was just tolerated and not acknowledged. It is only Michael the Brave who reinstates it as a religion in its own right by establishing the Mitropoly in Alba Iulia. Moreoever, Michael the Brave signs the anti-Ottoman treaty with Prince Sigismund Bathory in Alba Iulia in 1595 on condition that the Orthodox religion is acknowledged and respected. The newly acquired status is soon lost, though, with the death of the great voivode and the dissipation of his political ideals. However, the Mitropoly represented by the Metropolitan of Ardeal, Ioan from Prislop, continues its activities.

4.1 The history of the 17th century and the Şchei neighborhood of Braşov

The 17th century is a time of instability when the rulers from across the mountains show their support for the princes from Ardeal and establish political and defensive alliances. In line with the direction initiated by Michael the Brave, the ruler of Wallachia, Radu Şerban, is asked for his support between 1611 and 1613 by Prince Gabriel Bathory in his fight against the armed forces of the nobles gathered around Moise Szekely. This is the time a treaty is signed. With a view to that, Leon Tomşa, ruler of Moldova and Radu Mihnea, ruler of Wallachia meet in Braşov in 1616. While staying in the town they also encounter the Romanians from Şchei and attend the Orthodox Liturgy in the Church of Saint Nicholas. In 1635, Matei Basarab and Gheorghe Rakozy forge an alliance and three years later, the latter allies with the ruler of Moldova, Vasile Lupu. A similar policy is to be pursued by Prince Rakozy II who forms alliances with Gheorghe Ştefan of Moldova and with Constantin Şerban of Wallachia.

Relationships like the ones outlined above place the town of Braşov in the middle of events as a place where the messages to and from Alba Iulia first arrive, the contacts with the other Romania rulers are established, refuge is granted and the messengers of the new ruler first arrive.

According to Iorga, in the 17th century "every appointment of a new ruler, every change in the ruling system triggers jail time, torture, or imprisonment time in the pit – the defeated would rather go to Sibiu than come to Braşov, but they have to go through the town where the messengers announcing the new ruler also arrive."[56]

---

56 Iorga Nicolae, *Braşovul şi românii, (Romanian for Braşov and the Romanians),* Bucureşti, 1905, p. 230.

The services of the priests and school teachers from Şchei are valued by the Saxons because of their knowledge of the Romanian language and hence are paid separately. It is exactly this knowledge and the services provided in this respect by representatives of the Romanian community in Şchei that shields their rights.

The first information on the messages dispatched between the Braşov and the other two Romanian countries goes back to the second half of the 15th century: in 1477 priest Costea takes a message to Liotă Basarab, ruler of Wallachia; in 1484 priest Coman runs errands to Vlad Călugărul; around 1535 priest Petru from Şchei is sent as a messenger to Petru Rareş; in 1545 priest Toma dispatches communiqués to Mircea Ciobanu; in 1554 priest Dobre from Şchei takes missives to Pătraşcu cel Bun and to Alexandru Lăpuşneanu. It is another priest, protopope Mihai that the Saxons rely on to convey their message to Michael the Brave, urging him to spare the villages around Braşov from looting and destruction. In 1611, Vasile, chronicler and priest, is sent by the functionary of Braşov, Michael Weiss, to the court of Radu Şerban in Wallachia to ask him to send his troops to Transylvania to support the Saxons.

These contacts and messages are beneficial for the school teachers and priests in Şchei since they enlarge their horizons and access to information. They argue in favor of the school and church in Şchei in front of the Romanian rulers and always return with donations in money or valuable items. Through their actions they manage to represent official interests, as well as to serve the interests of the Romanian community in Şchei. Most of the trips are made on political grounds. Thus, for example, in the 17th century Vasile, chronicler and priest, represents the interests of the church in front of Matei Basarab and Vasile Lupu.

As part of the political relations, Braşov is a refuge for rulers and their court, as it is the case of Mircea cel Bătrân in 1395 and the boyards accompanying him. In 1447, Iancu of Hunedoara sends a letter to the community from Braşov regarding a house belonging to Vladislav from Wallachia, a relative of his. Laiotă Basarab spends the last part of his life in Braşov and in 1481 is buried in the portico of the Church of Saint Nicholas. Matei Aga, before he becomes a ruler, wanders around Transylvania and spends some time in Braşov. In the 17th century, the Canatacuzino family buys the Recea estate, near Făgăraş, while Mihai Cantacuzino owns a whole village, Budila. His brother, aga Bălăceanu, leaves his daughters in Braşov for security reasons. The wife of Şerban herself, Păuna, asks for refuge in one of the church cells in Şchei, dies in 1646 and is buried in this neighborhood in 1709. Gheorghe Cantacuzino lives in Braşov and organizes his wedding in this town in 1709. In 1679, Velicico Costin, the brother of Miron Costin, goes through Braşov.

Most of the information available on the people who at one time in their life live or pass through the town is related to Constantin Brâncoveanu, a ruler who maintained good relations both with the Saxons from Braşov and with the Romanians in Şchei. Under the uncertain and troubled conditions of the 17th century he seeks refuge in Braşov. At the beginning of his rule, in order to mitigate the plans and plots of the Wallachian boyars wandering around Transylvania, he asks them to return to Wallachia, promising them their reinstatement. During the first months of his administration he negotiates with the Saxons from Braşov to purchase plots of land to build houses in Şchei. Both the Cantacuzino and Brâncoveanu families granted loans to the Saxons which indebted them. In 1678, before becoming a ruler, Brâncoveanu comes to Braşov in order to convince the Cantacuzino family: his mother, Stanca, Pârvu Cantacuzino and his cousin Teodor Balş, the son in law of Pârvu, to return to Bucureşti. For fear he might be removed from rule by the Ottoman Empire, he takes refuge in Braşov in 1707, but when the rumors prove wrong he returns to Bucureşti. However, he negotiates the purchase of some houses and "in order to avoid roving Brâncoveanu obtains from the Austrian War Council an agreement to be hosted between 1701–1707"[57]. With the support of two diplomats from Şchei, David Corbea and Teodor Corbea, he manages to buy two Saxon houses exempted from taxes, as well as a house in Bartolomeu, a neighborhood of Braşov. As far as the two Corbea brothers are concerned, they are really appreciated by Brâncoveanu and the school in Şchei plays an important role in their education. Another important contribution of Brâncoveanu to the Şchei community is his role in obtaining rights for the Romanian merchants from this district.

---

57 Vasile Oltean, *Brâncoveanu- văzut prin documentele din Şchei* (Romanian for *Brâncoveanu as presented by the documents from Şchei*) in "Astra", no. 12, 1972, p. 17.

His houses in Şchei are ready to accommodate him all the time. In this respect, "when Brâncoveanu is banished from rule and taken to Constantinople, the boxes from the houses in Şchei are open to make an inventory of the goods and many valuables are discovered"[58]. After his death, his direct descendants are to live in these houses, namely Lady Ancuţa and her husband, Lady Bălaşa and Manolache Lambru, as well as Lady Brâncoveanu.

Both the Romanian rulers and the high ranking priests from across the mountains show concern and support for the situation of the Romanians in Şchei in various ways. In this respect, there are two types of networking and ongoing relationships established by the Şchei community: on one hand, the relations with Wallachia and Moldova; on the other hand, the ones with the surrounding areas. Moreover, in terms of the features of these relationships, they can be further broken down into three levels: political relations with the Romanian and Transylvanian rulers within which the Saxons also play a part; relations of the church with Romanian rulers and high ranking priests, of a low intensity and yet not unimportant; cultural links between Şchei and the surrounding areas.

Braşov is a stopover for the messengers sent by high ranking officials from Moldova and Wallachia to the capital city of Transylvania. Serafim is the first messenger mentioned by the records of Braşov who, on August 10th 1585 is sent by Mircea Turcitul to negotiate with the Saxons some administrative issues. Starting with the 17th century the town records provide more information that is confirmed by Tempea's chronicle. Thus, in March 1606, these documents mention the presence of Luca, the Metropolitan of Ungrovlahia (that is Wallachia or "Wallachia near Hungary") along with that of Metropolitan Teoctist of Bălgrad in order to mediate a conflict between the priest Neogoslav, serving in Şchei, even though he was not a local by birth, and the other priests who demanded his removal from the priesthood for having disregarded a local tradition. Other important figures who stop in Braşov while travelling in Transylvania for various reasons are: in 1632, Metropolitan Grigorie (1629–1632) of Ungrovlahia is sent by Leon Vodă to Alba Iulia and when returning he meets the Şchei

58 Nicolae Iorga, *Op. cit.*, p. 235.

community representatives; in May 1640, Matei Basarab, the Wallachian ruler, on his way back from Alba Iulia where he dispatches a message to Rakozi II, goes through Braşov; Ignatie Sârbul (1653–1656), Metropolitan of Ungrovlahia, visits the town twice – once, in 1655, when he is sent by Constantin Şerban to ask the support of Rakozy II to defeat the mutiny of the pedestrian mercenaries in charge of guarding the Wallachian ruler's court, and the second time, in 1659, while serving the ruler Mihnea III, he is sent to Rakozy II to conclude an anti-Ottoman treaty with him.

The Şchei neighborhood of Braşov also serves as a refuge for church high representatives. Thus, in 1672, the house of Vasile, brother in law of protopope Vâlcu, hosts the future Metropolitan of Wallachia, Varlaam, along with another person by the name of Ioasaf.

One eloquent example of the relations between Şchei and the regions from across the mountains is that with the Mitropoly of Ungrovlahia. Ever since the 15th century, the title of the Wallachian metropolitans includes the phrase meaning "exarch of the highlands" that refers to the mountainous regions of Wallachia, but also to the areas in southern Transylvania. Moreover, the anointment of the priests from Braşov is done in Wallachia before and even after the establishment of the Mitropoly of Ardeal is headquartered in Bălgrad. All of the above is proof of the forethought for the spiritual well-being of the Orthodox from Transylvania. Paul of Aleppo, while crossing the three Romanian countries notes the following: "almost all peasants from around Braşov are of Orthodox faith; their bishops are under the jurisdiction of the Wallachian metropolitan. There are more than 1,500 priests..."[59]. The geographical positioning of Braşov is actually one of the major factors for such close relationships. In this respect, it is worth recalling that the church in Şchei is entirely built with donations made by Wallachian rulers.

4.2 Donations for the church and school in Şchei

The first donations to the Şchei community come from Vlad Călugărul around 1490 and are used to build the wooden church. Neagoe Basarab

59 Apud, Mircea Păcurariu, *Legăturile bisericii ortodoxe din Transilvania cu Ţara Românerască şi Moldova în secolelel XVI–XVIII* (The Relations of the Orthodox Church from Transylvania with Wallachia and Moldova between the 16th–18th Centuries), Sibiu, 1968, p. 5.

(1512–1521) contributes both materially and conceptually to the construction of the stone church. Moreover, Petru Cercel makes a donation to support the raising of the front pillars of the above mentioned church. Aron Vodă, ruler of Moldova, upon the request made by protopope Mihai, contributes 12,000 Turkish silver coins for the construction of a school building.

The relations established between the church in Şchei with the Mitropoly from Wallachia do not transform the former into an ancillary of the latter. On the contrary, these are the means by which the rulers and metropolitans from Wallachia manage to morally support the Romanian Orthodox community from across the mountains. As already indicated, the anointment of the priests serving in the Şchei parish is done in Wallachia and becomes a tradition in its own right. For example, in 1659, when protopope Vasile dies, Ioan Corbea and Vasile Hoban apply for the vacancy. Since both of them come from Şchei and hence meet a major requirement made for the priests serving this community, they are both anointed in Bucureşti. The evidence that these relations are beneficial for the spiritual well-being and growth of the Orthodox from Transylvania is the stance adopted by the priests from the Bârsa County along with those in Şchei against Athanasie Anghel's (Transylvanian metropolitan) arguments in favor of the Union with the Roman Catholic Church.

In 1701, Vasile Grid, the protopope, writes a letter to Teodosie, metropolitan of Wallachia, recommending the appointment a Chancery writer by the name of Petcu so that he can be appointed priest in the church from Satulung. Consequently, Petcu goes to the Mitropoly from Bucureşti where he spends several days in order to learn how to perform religious services. The same metropolitan anoints a number of priests: in 1706, Oprea, Vasile Grid's brother, who is to serve as priest in Şchei and in 1713, deacon Ioan, the son of Petru Cărăuşu. The protopopes and priests in Şchei play a major role in safeguarding the preservation of Orthodox traditions around Braşov, as well as in recommending priests for anointment. That proves the full acknowledgment of the salient role played by the church in Şchei by Wallachian metropolitans. In this respect, Tempea notes that in 1692, the future metropolitan of Ardeal, while travelling to Bucureşti stops in Braşov and requires two of the priests in Şchei, Vasile Grid and Oprea to accompany him on his journey.

As part of the relations established with a view to preserving the Orthodox traditions, the priests from Şchei also travel to Moscow during the 17th century. For example, priest Oprea goes twice to the court of the Russian czar: in 1685 and from 1690–1692, and protopope Vasile Hoban travels to Moscow in 1697. The latter's mission is of a major importance since, at the time, the Orthodox tradition encounters a number of challenges. Consequently, "he asks for the support of Peter the Great and receives 20 rubles and a Slavonic Ochtoechos"[60] and during his long stay in Moscow he is well treated.

The church in Şchei owns great riches in the 17th century. It is the prototope's residence and the religious services there are performed by five or six priests. Religious and blood ties favor important donations to this establishment: in 1602 Nicolae Pătraşcu bequeathes the Micşuneşti estate; in 1748, Dumitraşcu, son of Vlaicu Budişteanu, donates the Budişeni estate; in 1750, Smaranda Bălăceanu, niece of Consatantin Bălăceanu endows the church with eight acres of vineyards and two estates in Buzău county. Apart from the donations made to the church in Şchei there are many others directed towards other churches from the Bârsa County. For example, Neagoe Basarab built a church in Zărneşti in 1515; the Recea monastery is raised with the full support of the Cantacuzino family; Constantin Brâncoveanu, contributes to the establishment of the Sâmbăta de Sus monastery and the church from Făgăraş.

Books play an important role in outlining the relations established among the three Romanian countries, as well as in supporting the Romanian Orthodox in preserving their religion against the pressures made by the Calvinist or Catholic movements. Thus, in the 17th century, when the printing activities from Bălgrad are rather inconsistent, the presses in Wallachia and Moldova meet the book demands coming from Tranyslvania. Books reached this country in various ways: by donations made by rulers, boyars, metropolitans and high ranking church representatives on occasions like anointments or purchases made by the Romanians from Ardeal who travel to Moldova or Wallachia.

---

60 Silviu Dragomir, *Relaţiile bisericii româneşti cu Rusia în veacul al XVII-lea,* (The Relations of the Orthodox Church with Russia in the 17th Century), Bucureşti, 1912, p. 67.

Petru Movilă, metropolitan of Kiev, also makes major contributions in books written in Greek and Romanian. In the first half of the 17th century he writes and issues a book entitled Mărturisire ortodoxă (Confession of the Orthodox Faith), an allegiance to the Orthodox religion and a guide to rely on in the face of Catholic pressures. Moreover, Varlaam, metropolitan of Moldova, writes Cazania (Homilies) in response to Catehismul calvinesc (The Calvinist Catechism). This is "not only an original and thoroughly documented work, but also a proof that the Orthodox Church representatives from the two countries are aware of their role in supporting the spiritual ties of Romanians"[61]. The same goal of countering Calvinist pressures is shared by Evanghelie învăţătoare (Gospel for Instruction) issued in Wallachia by Udrişte Năsturel. In his introductory remarks, he confesses that he wrote the book: "when I noticed that the people who are either too dumb or too benevolent and who, because of their sinful nature and uneducated simple minds, adopt teachings other than those of the true faith of God's church..."[62].

It is worth recalling that the Romanian rulers manifest their support not only in the spiritual area by encouraging book printing and dissemination in Transylvania, but also in the administrative domain by encouraging the accession to the position of Metropolitan of Bălgrad capable and trustworthy people concerned with the preservation of the Orthodox religion. For example, Vasile Lupu supports Ilie Iorest, who takes shelter in the Putna monastery against Calvinistic persecution. Moreover, four decades later, Şerban Cantacuzino aids Sava Brancovici, unjustly blamed and put on trial.

The use of the Romanian language both in writing/copying books and in performing religious service helps people's understanding.

The chroniclers of the time highlight the fact that the Romanian ethnic consciousness is shaped by the political, religious and spiritual relationships and administrative structures, as well as by the circulation of the books printed in the Romanian Cyrillic alphabet. This is also reflected in

61 Mircea Păcurariu, *op.cit.*, p. 37.

62 Candid Muşlea, *Istoria bisericii Sfântul Nicolae din Şcheii Braşovului* (Romanian for *The History of Saint Nicholas Churchfrom Şchei, Braşov*), Braşov, 1943, p. 283.

their chronicles: Ion Neculce refers to territories inhabited by Romanians, Radu Popescu is aware of the events taking place in neighboring Moldova, and Radu Temea presents events from the countries in parallel as if there was no distinction among them whatsoever.

Books are also exchanged within private groups. In this respect, the priests from around Şchei gather at the protopope's residence on various occasions (celebrations or burials), as it is the case with the funerals of protopope Vâlcu.

An important part of the cultural relationships among the Romanian provinces is the exchange of typographers. Coresi's decision to come to Braşov and establish printing is by no means a random one. On the contrary, it is grounded in the well-established tradition of the people from here to read and write in the Romanian language. Recent research in the field unveils that the priests from Şchei "take the initiative to print books on Coresi's press and actually they are its real owners"[63]. The school of copyists in Şchei makes its own contribution to the growth and preservation of Romanian culture. In this respect, after Coresi's departure this school continues printing books needed by the school and church. Some of the school representatives in the 17th century are: the priest Vasile, a copyist and chronicler of the time; Vasii Hoban, school teacher, priest, author of numerous manuscripts and also margin notes; Radu Tempea, a scholar and well known defender of the orthodox religion.

All of the above emphasizes the role of Şchei as a landmark in the relations of the territories on the two sides of the Carpathian Mountains. Additionally, this role is also highlighted by the cases of people in Şchei who become monks in monasteries from Wallachia: the priest Toma din Şchei takes the oath as monk in the Râncăciov monastery from Wallachia under the name of Timotei; Ioan Corbea, son of the two Humanist scholars – David and Teodor Corbea, takes the oath in the Sinaia monastery from Wallachia in 1670 under the name of Iosif.

A cultural tradition passed on from generation to generation within the families in Şchei is that young people continue their parents' activity in school or church. Those who graduate from the school in Şchei are sent to

63 Mircea Păcurariu, op.cit., p. 103.

further their education in Wallachia or in Serbia under the condition that they return to Şchei. Radu Temea II and Ioan Duma, son of Radu Duma the priest, are cases of people who take courses in Bucureşti and then return to Şchei. Other traditions worth noting are the anointment of priests in Wallachia, the regular visits of priests in Şchei to Moldova, Wallachia or even Moscow, as well as the messages on behalf of the Saxon authorities from Braşov dispatched by the priests in Şchei. These are irrefutable arguments that support the idea of close cultural and political relations among the three Romanian countries of Transylvania, Wallachia and Moldova.

Conclusions

The margin notes made in old books provide information that is important for fields like classical history, history of mentalities and perceptions, geopolitics and cultural studies since they reflect aspects related to habitats, socio-economic features of specific areas and communities, social categories such as the elites holding the power to influence the whole community and culturally influential leaders. This book is based on the information provided by the 17th century documents belonging to the Romanian community in Şchei that are now in the archives of Braşov. These documents have never been republished, which lends originality to the current endeavor. Out of 44 documents analyzed, 29 contain margin notes, whereas 14 bear no annotations whatsoever. Even though there are much more documents in the inventory dating back to the 17th century, they could not be consulted because of their deteriorated condition before being included in the archives or because of damage resulting from fire.

The information gathered upon the consultation of the above mentioned documents is organized in four chapters.

The **introductory chapter** outlines the most important, as well as the most recent research on old Romanian books that are archived in various places in Romania that underpin the guidelines for this book. In this respect, there are two major contributions worth noting: those of Nicolae Iorga and the team from the Romanian Academy.

Nicolae Iorga focuses his research on areas rich in old Romanian books. Concerning the old books from Transylvania and, more specifically, the ones from around and from within Braşov, he publishes two studies: "Braşovul şi românii. Scrisori şi lămuriri" ("Braşov and the Romanians. Letters and Explanations") published in Bucureşti in 1905 and "Scrisori şi inscripţii ardelene şi maramureşene" ("Letters and Inscriptions from Ardeal and Maramureş" issued in 1906 and subsequently included in the volume entitled *Studii şi documente privind istoria românilor* ("Studies and documents on Romanian History"). The information provided in this refers to the circulation of the books originating from Wallachia in Transylvania. He also writes a two volume book titled *Inscripţii din bisericile României* ("Inscriptions from Romania's churches") Bucureşti,

1905–1908, and *Inscripții și însemnări dinbisericile Iașului* ("Inscriptions and Annotations from the Churches in Iași") București 1907.

The team of the Romanian Academy assembled upon the initiative of Ioan Bianu, Nerva Hodoş and Dan Simonescu managed to gather information on old Romanian books dating back to the 15th, 17th and 18th centuries that can be found in various archives or collections and published the three volume book entitled *Bibliografia românească veche* ("Old Romanian Bibliography") before World War II. Additionally, a synthetic work on the books printed in Bucharest and the development of typographic activities is published by Barbu Teodorescu under the title of *Cartea veche românească 1508–1830* ("The Old Romanian Books between *1508–1830").*

Chapter II focuses on two directions. First, it analyzes the data on the history of the Church of Saint Nicholas and the school, two establishments of major importance for the Romanian community in Şchei and for all the Romanians from the south of Transylvania. Then, the chapter highlights the role played by the dynasties of priests and school teachers in passing on the legacy of books and the Orthodox religion. Some representative names of families in Şchei Braşov are: the Hobans, the Bărans, the Grids, the Corbeas, the Tempeas and the Dumas. Their members contributed to establishing the school in Şchei (known later by the name of The First School in the Romanian Language) in the 14th century, served as priests in the Church of Saint Nicholas, as messengers of the Romanians from Transylvania to the rulers from across the mountains, as well as translators and delegates on behalf of the Saxon authorities from Braşov in the relations between them and Wallachia or Moldova. They also supported and continued Coresi's activity in Braşov and thus contributed to the shaping of the Romanian language. All these scholars managed to preserve Romanian identity, culture and the Orthodox religion by taking a stance against pressures like the initiative related to the Union with the Roman Catholic Church launched in 1700.

Chapter III entitled **MARGIN NOTES IN OLD ROMANIAN BOOKS – A HISTORICAL SOURCE** is an analysis of the archive books bearing margin notes. These have not been published before and hence this book provides original and unedited information.

Romanian old books dating back to the 17th century are mostly written in Cyrillic Romanian. Very few are written in Slavonic. That testifies to the important role acquired by Romanian over Greek or Slavonic in that century. Apart from these, there are also books in German, Latin, Greek and French. However, they do not have any margin notes and, as a result, they are only listed in the first part of appendices. The lack of annotations in these books may be an indicator that French or German were not studied in the school in Şchei, even though the priests and school educators could speak German since they had to work with the Saxon authorities. However, these foreign languages were studied by children of German origin in the high school established by Johanes Honterus in Braşov. The books in the inventory are mostly of a religious nature since secular books first become more widespread with the 18th century.

Manuscripts are an important part of the documents dating back to the 17th century and are the result of the work done in the school of copyists in Şchei. Even though not all copyists' names are known to this day, their contribution is an important one in the cultural legacy of Şchei. Additionally, in the archives there are books printed in Râmnic, Govora or Bucureşti.

The content of the margin notes is varied and includes the name and position of the person making the note, mention of historical events, information on the history of the book and the attempt to portray local history. Both the printed book and the manuscript have a twofold function: as a means of performing religious service and as textbooks used for teaching reading and writing.

The margin notes introduce the reader into the world of priests and school teachers from the Bârsa County, as well as into that of common people who, at a given moment in time, had access to books. Only some of them are made known by other studies or works in the field and hence they augment the list of priests and school teachers known so far. These margin notes show a certain shyness of people towards books, their concern with recording in the margin notes only what is of importance to be known by this means, the value assigned to books unveiled by the severity of the curses for book theft and estrangement or the oath made to respect the moral values of the community in Şchei. Book costs are quite high for those times, equaling the value of half a hectare of land or of a pair of oxen (in the Middle Ages that was the equivalent of the dowry a girl would get from her parents).

Education is part of family legacy in Şchei. The Romanian community in this neighborhood is very well organized, consisting of very rich and influential merchants, as well as of craftsmen whose historical importance and rights are acknowledged by the Saxons. The wealth of this community is increased by donations in books, money and precious objects made to the church by the rulers and metropolitans from across the mountains as a result of their close relationships with the Romanians from Transylvania, and Şchei, in particular.

The margin notes disclose important information on the mentality of people, on their attitude to education and books, on the role played by the church in preserving moral principles underpinning community life and, most importantly, on the fact that books are so valuable that they are viewed as a legacy for future generations.

The 17th century represents a landmark for the Romanian culture and traditions and of which Braşov is a highpoint. Important contributions to this are made by the school of copyists in Şchei, by the support given by the 16th century priests to Coresi's actions, as well as by the stance adopted by the priests in Şchei against the Union of the Orthodox Church with the Roman Catholic Church promoted in Ardeal.

Chapter IV describes the role of the Romanian neighborhood of Braşov in the political changes characteristic of the 17th century, as well as the part played by the church in Şchei in consolidating the Romanian community as a result of the numerous donations made by the Romanian rulers and boyars. Braşov is at the crossroads of commercial trade routes to Wallachia and from there on to the Ottoman Empire or to Western Europe through the Hungarian and Austrian Empires. Commercial relations are thus a means that facilitates cultural and religious exchanges. Moreover, the relations with the Romanian rulers from across the mountains, the delegations of priests and school teachers in Şchei travelling to Ukraine and Moscow are constant. All of the above factors explain the significant number of old books that can be found in the archive form Şchei, Braşov.

In conclusion, the information provided by this book replenishes the data on the local history of the school and church in Şchei, Braşov, as well provides insights about the people who worked closely with books by analyzing unedited archive documents that have not been used by other researchers in the field.

Bibliography

A. Sources

1. Inedited

Old Romanian books dating back to the 17th century in the inventory of the archives of the First School in Romanian Language in Şchei, Braşov (coded as doc.no..,(document no.) in the text and that corresponds to the information provided in the appendices).

2. Edited

Bogdan Ioan (1905) *Documente şi regeste privitoare la relaţiile Ţări Româneşti cu Braşovul şi Ungaria* (*Documents and records on the relations of Wallachia with Braşov and Hungary*), Institutul de arte grafice "Carol Göbl"(Institute of graphic arts): Bucureşti,.

Bot Livia, Octavian Şchiau (1960) *Radu Tempea-Istoria sfintei besearici a Şcheilor Braşovului* (*Radu Tempea- The History of the Holy Church in Şchei, Braşov*), Publishing House pentru Literatură (Publishing House for Literature): Bucureşti.

Stinghe Sterie (1899) *Istoria sfintei biserici a Şceilor Braşovului- Manuiscript de la Radu Tempea* (The History of the Holy Church in Şchei, Braşov – A Manuscript of Radu Tempea), Ciurcu Publishing House: Braşov.

Quellen zur Geschichte der Stadt Brasso, vol. I-VII, Braşov, 1866–1925.

B. General Bibliography

Albu Nicolae (1944) *Istoria învăţământului românesc din Transilvania până la 1800*, (*The History of Education in the Romanian Language in Transylvania until 1800*), Lumina Typography: Blaj.

Bianu Ioan, Hodoş Nerva, Simionescu Dan (1903–1944) *Bibliografia românească veche*, (*Old Romanian Bibliography*), vol. I–IV, Academy's Publishing House: Bucureşti.

Cartojan Nicolae (1980) *Istoria literaturii române vechi* (*The History of Old Romanian Literature*), Minerva Publishing House: Bucureşti, 1980.

(1961) *Din istoria Transilvaniei,*(*Excerpts from the History of Transylvania*) vol. I–II, Publishing House Academy's: Bucureşti.

Dragomir Silviu (1912) *Relaţiile biserici româneşti cu Rusia în veacul al XVIl-lea,* (*The Relations of the Romanian Orthodox Church with Russia in the 17th Century*), Bucureşti.

Iorga Nicolae (1929–1932) *Istoria bisericii româneşti şi a vieţii religioase a românilor* (*The History of the Romanian Orthodox Church and of Romanian's Religious Life*), vol. I–II, Bucureşti.

Iorga Nicolae Istoria literaturii religioase a românilor până la 1688 (*The History of Romanian's Religious Lietrature until 1688*), Bucureşti.

Iorga Nicolae (1964) *Istoria literaturii româneşti vechi* (*The History of Old Romanian Literature*), Academy's Publishing House: Bucureşti.

Iorga Nicolae (1989) *Istoria românilor din Ardeal şi Ungaria* (*The History of Romanians from Ardeal and Hungary*), Scientific and Encyclopedic Publishing House: Bucureşti.

Iorga Nicolae (1902) *Sate şi preoţi din Ardeal* (*Villages and Priests from Ardeal*), "Carol Göbl" Arts Institute: Bucureşti.

Lupaş Ioan (1941) *Cărturari şi istorici români din Transilvania* (*Romanian Scholars and Historians from Transylvania*), vol. I–II, Romanian Writing Publishing House: Craiova.

Meteş Stefan, Din relaţiile noastre cu Rusia (*On Our Relations with Russia*) in "Mitropolia Ardealului" (*The Mitropoly of Ardeal*), no. 11–12, pp. 837–863.

Meteş Stefan (1934) *Domnii din principatele române pribegi în Transilvania în veacul 18th* (*Rulers from the Romanian Countries Taking Refuge in Transylvania in the 18th Century*), Romanian Book Typography: Cluj.

Meteş Stefan (1935) *Istoria bisericii şi a vieţii religioase a românilor din Transilvania şi Ungaria* (*The History of the Orthodox Church and of Romanians' Religious Life in Transylvania and Hungary*), Sibiu.

Meteş Stefan (1926) *Mănăstiri româneşti din Transilvania şi Ungaria* (*Romanian Monasteries from Transylvania and Hungary*), vol. I–II, Sibiu.

Meteş Stefan, (1915) *Şerban vodă Cantacuzino şi biserica românească din Ardeal* (*Şerban vodă Cantacuzino and the Romanian Orthodox Church from Ardeal*), Vălenii de Munte.

Păcurariu Mircea (1968) *Legăturile bisericii ortodoxe din Transilvania cu Ţara Românească şi Moldova în secolele XVI–18th* (*The Relations of the Orthodox Church with Wallachia and Moldova between the* 16th *and 18th Centuries*), Sibiu.

Păcurariu Mircea (1981) *Istoria bisericii ortodoxe române* (*The History of the Romanian Orthodox Church)*, vol. I–III, The Biblical and Missionary Institute of Romanian Orthodox Church Publishing House.

Schiau Octavian, (1978) *Cărturari şi cărţi în spaţiu românesc medieval* (*Scholars and Bookswithin the Medieval Romanian Area*), Cluj-Napoca, Dacia Publishing House.

Ştrempel Gabriel (1878) *Copişti de manuscrise româneşti până la 1800* (*Copiysts of Romanian Manuscripts until 1800*), vol. I–II, Academy's Publishing House: Bucureşti.

Tomescu Mircea (1968) *Istoria cărţii româneşti de la începuturi până la 1918* (*The History of Romanian Books from Beginning until 1918*), Scientific Publishing House: Bucureşti.

C. Specialised Bibliogaphy

Arbore Petru Vergiliu, *Însemnări culese de pe marginea cărţilor bisericeşti din oraşul Focşani* (*Margin Notes Compiled in Religious Books from Focşani Town*), in "Milcovia", 1931, vol II, pp. 237–247, vol. III pp. 56–66, 1931, vol. IV, pp. 54–64.

Barbu Bucur Sebastian (1975) *Ioan Sin Radu Duma Braşoveanu* in "Biserica ortodoxă română" (*The Romanian Orthodox Church*), pp. 100–106.

Bârseanu Andrei (1902) *Istoria şcoalelor centrale greco-catolice din Braşov* (*The History of Greek Catholic Schools from Braşov*), Ciurcu Typography: Braşov.

Bârlea Ioan (1909) *Însemnări din bisericile Maramureşului* (*Margin Notes in the Books from Maramureş Churches)*, Academy's Publishing House: Bucureşti.

Chiţimia Ioan, *Din vechea răspândire a cărţilor româneşti din Ţara Oltului* (*On the Dissemination of Romanian Books in the Olt County*), in "Mitropoly of Oltenia", no. 5–6, 1970, pp. 534–542.

Corfus Ilie (1975) *Însemnări de demult* (*Margin Notes of Yester Time*), Publishing House Junimea: Iaşi.

Dreghiciu Doina, *Cartea românească de pe valea Sebeşului* (*The Romanian Books from the Sebeş Valley*), in "Apulum", no. 19th, 1981, pp. 487–498, 1982, pp. 534–542.

Dudaş Florin (1977) *Cartea veche românească în Bihor* (*Old Romanian Books from Bihor*), Oradea.

Iorga Nicolae (1905) *Braşovul şi românii* (*Braşov and the Romanians*), Stabilimentul grafic I. V. Savu: Bucureşti.

Iorga Nicolae (1905–1908) *Inscripţii din bisericile României* (*Inscriptions from Romania's Churches*), vol. I–II, Bucureşti.

Iorga Nicolae (1907) *Inscripţii şi însemnări din bisericile Iaşului* (Inscriptions and Annotations from the Churches in Iaşi), Bucureşti.

Iorga Nicolae, *Însemnări de cronică ale clericilor din Şcheii Braşovului* (*Chronicle Annotations of the Priests in Şchei, Braşov*), in "Buletinul Comisiei Istorice a României" (*The Bulletin of Romania's Historical Board*), vol. XII, 1933, pp. 60–99.

Iorga Nicolae (1906) *Scrisori şi inscripţii ardelene şi maramureşene* (*Letters and Inscriptions from Ardeal and Maramureş*), in "Studii şi documente privind istoria românilor" (*"Studies and Documents on Romanian History"*), Bucureşti.

Iorga Nicolae, *Socotelile Braşovului şi scrisori româneşti către sfat în secolul al 17th-lea* (*The 18th Century Records of Braşov and Romania Letters to the Council*), "Carol Göbl" Arts Institute: Bucureşti, 1889.

Lacea Constantin (1909) *Biblioteca veche a bisericii Sfântul Nicolae din Braşov* (*The Old Library of the Church of Saint Nicholas from Braşov*), in "Transilvania", no. 1, January-March, pp. 100–106.

Lacea Constantin (1943) *Contribuții la cunoașterea trecutului și educației vechilor meseriași și negustori brașoveni* (*Information on the History and Education of the Old Craftsmen and Merchants from Brașov*), Brașov.

Idem, *Trocar*, ,in "The Bârsa Countyi", May-June 1931, no. 3, pp. 234–237.

Leu Valeria, *Circulația cărții românești în valea Almăjului până la 1840* (*The Circulation of Romanian Books in the Almăj Valley until 1840*), in "Banatica", 1979, pp. 467–483.

Literat Valeriu (1938) *Din Țara Oltului. Însemnări vechi din biserici noi* (*Old Margin Notes from New Churches in the Olt County*), Brașov.

Liu Nicolae, *Cartea cu însemnări manuscris* (*Books with Handwritten Margin Notes*), in "Studii și cercetări de documente și bibliografie" (*Studies and Research on Documents and Bibliography*), no. 2–3, 1967, pp. 305–321.

Mârza Eva, *Cărți românești pe valea Oltului* (*Romanian Books in the Olt Valley*), in "Apulum", no. 17, 1979, pp. 342–367.

Meteș Ștefan, *Cronica popei Vasile din Scheii Brașovului* (*The Chronicle of Priest Vasile in Șchei, Brașov*), in "Drum drept" (*Straight Road*), Vălenii de Munte, no. 3, 1913, pp. 165–188.

Molin Virgil, *Aria de răspândire a cărților de Râmnic în Banat în secolul al 17th-lea* (*The Dissemination Area of Books from Râmnic in Banat in the 17th century*), in "The Mitropoly of Muntenia", no. 11–12, 1967, pp. 859–869.

Mureșianu A. Aurel (1931) *Lucruri nouă în trecutul românilor brașoveni. Un dascăl brașovean necunoscut în veacul 17th* (*New Information on the History of Romanians from Brașov. An Anonymous School Teacher of Brașov in the 17th Century*), in "The Bârsa County", no. 6, October-November, pp. 500–505.

Mureșianu A. Aurel, *Un împiedecător al avântului național al românilor brașoveni* de acum *200 de ani: popa Teodor Băran* (*Priest Teodor Băran: a Fighter against (for?) the National Ideals Shared by the Romanians from Brașov 200 Years Ago*), in "The Bârsa County", no. 3, May-June 1930, pp. 204–207.

Muşlea Candid (1943) *Biserica Sfântul Nicolae din Şcheii Braşovului* (*the Church of Saint Nicholas in Şchei, Braşov*), vol. I–II, Astra Graphic Arts Institute: Braşov.

Muşlea Candid, *Însemnările popei Nicolae Grid despre Şcheii Braşovului de altă dată şi biserica lor* (*Priest Nicolae Grid's Margin Notes on the Past Şchei, Braşov and the Church from Here*), in "The Bârsa County", July-August 1931, pp. 341–352.

Muşlea Candid, *O anchetă în Scheii Braşovului la anul 1751* (*An Investigation in Şchei, Braşov in 1751*), in "The Bârsa County", no. 5, September-October 1930, pp. 100–103.

Muşlea Candid (1939) *O dinastie de preoţi şi protopopi: Radu Temea* (*Radu Temea-A dynasty of Priests and Prototopes*), Bucureşti.

Idem, *Protopopul Eustatie Grid* (*Eustatie Grid, the Protopope*), Braşov, 1939.

Nicolae, Metropolitan of Ardeal (1980) *Biserica ortodoxă română una şi aceeaşi în toate timpurile* (*The Everlasting Unchanged Romanian Orthodox Church*), Sibiu.

Nussbächer Gernot (1981) *Das Urkunden und Chroniken*, Publishing House Kriterion: Bucureşti.

Oltean Vasile (1981) *Acte, documente şi scrisori din Şcheii Braşovului* (*Deeds, Documents and Letters from Şchei, Braşov*), Minerva Publishing House: Bucureşti.

Oltean Vasile, *Brâncoveanu văzut prin documentele din Şchei* (*Brâncoveanu as Depicted by Documents in Şchei*), in "Astra", no. 12, 1972, p. 17.

Oltean Vasile, *Cronici şi cronicari din Şcheii Braşovului* (*Chronicles and Chroniclers from Şchei, Braşov*), in "Astra", no. 2, 1973, p. 14.

Oltean Vasile, *Descoperirea unui codice miscelaneu în limba română* (*The Discovery of a Miscellaneous Codex in the Romanian Language*), in Revista literară ("The Literary Magazine"), no. 5, 1975, p. 19.

Oltean Vasile, *Întâia şcoală românească* (*The First Romanian School*), Braşov, 1981.

Oltean Vasile, *Şcoala de copişti din Şchei* (*The School of Copyists in Şchei*), in "Astra", no. 4, 1980, pp. 12–13.

Oltean Vasile (1989) *Şcoala românească din Şcheii Braşovului* (*The School in Romanian Language in Şchei*), Scientific and Encyclopedic Publishing House: Bucureşti.

Oltean Vasile, *Semnificaţia documentului voievodal de la 1665 descoperit în Şcheii Braşovului* (*The Significance of the 1665 voivode's document discovered in Şchei, Braşov*), in "Astra", no. 7, 1989, p. 10.

Panait Cristache Ioana, *Cărţi vechi cu însemnări din bisericile mitropoliei Banatului* (*Old Books with Margin Notes from the Churches of Banat Mitropoly*), in "The Mitropoly of Banat", no. 6, 1969, pp. 289–291.

Panaitescu P. Petre (1960) *Începuturile scrisului în limba română* (*The Beginning of Writing in the Romanian Language*), in "Studii şi materiale de istorie medie" (*Middle Age Studies and Materials*), IV, pp. 150–185.

Panaitescu P. Petre (1922) *Însemnări din cărţile bisericeşti româneşti greco-orientale din Timişoara* (*Margin Notes in the Romanian Eastern Orthodox Church from Timişoara*), in "The Historical Magazine", pp. 201–202.

Păcurariu Mircea (1975) *Listele cronologice ale ierarhilor biserici ortodoxe române* (*The Chronological Lists of Romanian Orthodox Hierarchs*), Biblical Institute Publishing House: Bucureşti.

Pop Dariu, *Mărturii strămoşeşti. Note din cărţile bisericeşti sătmărene* (*Ancient Testimonies. Margin Notes in the Books from Sătmar Churches*), Satu Mare, 1938.

Prişcu Ioan, *Racoviţeştii îngropaţi la biserica Sf. Nicolae din Braşov* (*Members of the Racoviţeşti Family Buried in the Church of Saint Nicholas from Braşov*), in "The Romanian Telegraph", no. 63–64, pp. 91–96.

Prişcu Ioan, *Vechimea bisericii Sf. Nicolae din Şcheii Braşovului* (*On the History of the Church of Saint Nicholas in Şchei, Braşov*), in "The Bârsa County", no. 4, July-August 1931, pp. 339–341.

Râpă Buidiu Dan (1972–1973) *Cartea românească veche cu însemnări* (*Old Romanian Books with Margin Notes*), in,"Danubius", XI–XII, pp. 59–65.

Sever Alexe, *Suflete uitate –Boghicii* (*Uncommemorated Names: The Boghici's*), in "The Bârsa County", no. 4, 5, and 6, 1930, pp. 290–310.

Stinge Sterie (1901) *Documente privitoare la trecutul românilor din Şchei* (Romania for *Documents on the History of Romanians in Şchei*), vol. I–IV, Ciurcu Typography: Braşov.

Struţeanu Scarlat, Fraţii Corbea, doi umanişti ardeleni la curtea lui Constantin Brâncoveanu (*The Corbea Brothers – two Humanists from Ardeal at Constantin Brâncoveanu' s Court*), in "Ramuri", Craiova, no. 1–2, 1941, pp. 40–45.

Ştrempel Gabriel Manuscrisele româneşti aflate la Leningrad şi Kiev (*Romanian Manuscripts from Leningrad and Kiev*), in "Studii şi cercetări de bibliografie" (*Bibliographical Studies and Research*), XII, 1972, pp. 21–38.

Sulică Nicolae (1940) *Cea mai veche şcoală românească din cuprinsul României întregite* (*The Oldest Romanian School from Greater Romania*), Romanian Book Publishing House: Bucureşti.

Sulică Nicolae (1943) *Minunata cetatea a Braşovului-cărturari braşoveni ai secolului al XVI-lea, ca ctitori ai limbii noastre literare* (*The Wonderful Citadel of Braşov – XVI Century Scholars from Braşov*), Braşov.

Şchiau Octavian, Circulaţia Cazaniei lui Varlaam în Transilvania (*The Circultaion of Varlaam's Homilies in Transylvania*), in "Mitropoly of Oltenia", no. 5–6, pp. 524.

Appendices

A. Catalogue of the 17th century books from the Şchei archive

1. List of books from the Şchei archive with no margin notes
2. List of books with margin notes

B. Names of people recorded in the margin notes

1. Orthodox Romanian priests from Şchei (in chronological order)
2. Orthodox Romanian priests from around Braşov (in chronological order)
3. School teachers and copyists
4. Other people

C. Alphabetical index of places mentioned in book annotations

A. Catalogue of 17th Century Old Books from Şchei, Braşov

A.1 Archived Books with no Margin Notes

The History of Varlaam and Ioasaf (Inventory no. 93)

Slavonic printed book, edited in Russia during the time of Petru Movilă (1597–1647), title page missing; 363 pages, 20x16 cm, wooden and leather binding

May and June Slavonic Menaion (Inventory no. 32)

17th century manuscript, 197 pages, 31.5x18 cm, wooden and leather binding.

Herodoti Halicarnassci historiarum libri IX (Inventory no. 1327)

Printed in Frankfurt, 1608, 712 pages, 35x22 cm, no binding.

Gospel's Interpretation

Printed in Kiev in 1636, 532 pages, 16 lines per page, wooden and velvet binding **Slavonic Hymn Book** (Inventory no. 89)

Printed in Kiev 1625, 109 pages, 20 x 16.8 cm, regular binding; it includes the homilies of John Chrysostom, (Inventory no. 1303).

Exposito patrum grecorum in psalmos

Printed in Venice, 1646, 2 volumes in Latin and Greek

Tistament de la Racoţi tiparnic (Testament from the Racoţi Typography) (Inventory no. 1597).

Printed in Alba Iulia, in 1648, damaged copy provided by Viştea de Jos.

Iohanne Latermanno, *Ceaneae theologorum ortodoxorum* (Inventory no. 760).

Dantisci printed book, 1648.

Corpus Biyantinae historiae (Inventory no. 1327).

Printed in Venice, in 1648, 1 volume.

Ioan Iacobus Weckenn, *De secretaris* (Inventory no. 1025).

Printed in 1662 provided by Ioan Petric, protopope of Braşov.

Alexander Rossen, *Unterschliedlicher Gottesdienste in der gantzen Welt* (Inventory no. 1026).

Printed in Heidelberg, 1674; 1040 pages, 10.5 x 17 cm, leather and cardboard binding.

Francois Turrethin, *Recueil de sermons sne divers textes de L'ecritures S. Pour l'etat present de l'eglise* (Inventory no. 1023).

Printed in Geneva, 1687, 734 pages, 17.2 x 10.8 cm.

The New Testament (Inventory no. 1465).

Printed in Frankfurt/ Main, 1692, written in Greek and edited by Rudolphus Leudnus, 304 pages, 17.5 x 11 cm, incomplete copy, cardboard binding.

Martin Luther, **Bible** (Inventory no. 1170),

Printed in Wittenberg, 1696, 230 pages, leather and cardboard binding.

Saint Macarius, **Homilies** (Inventory no. 974),

Unedited printing in German by Gottfied Arnold, 1696, 432 pages, leather and cardboard binding, 16.4 x 9.5 cm.

A.2 Books with margin notes

1. ROMANIAN CHANTS, SOME WRITTEN FOR LENT BY PRIEST VASILE AND OTHERS FOR THE WHOLE YEAR BY *MICUL CREȚUL*

Manuscript finished in 1613, 67 pages, 30.7 x 20.7 cm, leather and cardboard binding, inventory no. 36.

Margin note on page 30:

"I, Vasilie, son of priest Mihai of Braşov 7121(1613) wrote this".

2. *PHILOSOPHY TEXTBOOK*

Bilingual manuscript in Slavonic and Greek, 315 pages, 20 x 15.5 cm, sheepskin and cardboard binding, 25–27 lines per page, Inventory no. 43.

Margin note on page 139:

"I, Barbul, the school teacher, wrote this"

Margin note on page 307:

"I, Teoctist, hieromonk, copied this book of John Climacus and its interpretation and if I donate it before or after my death may it be for spiritual growth in monastery or in solitude, and may its contents remain unchanged and whoever will to take it from where I donate it shall never be forgiven by God, all saints or me, the sinner, Amen."

Margin note on page 1:

"I, Stanciul, wrote to you young Barbul and I pray for nothing but peace and health..."

Margin note on page 160:

"I, Rau Murgan, hereby take the pledge to guarantee for my brother in law, Costea, in front of priest protopope Văsii Hoban and the holy synod that in a year's time he will stop drinking wine, replenish his and his wife's house with things and food resulting from either their individual or collective work and respect his wife as a woman as she will respect him as a man. And he shall be held accountable for all of the above in front of Radu Murgan, the priest and the Holy Synod. And should he drink, I will expose his deeds to the priest and put him naked in a den for three days and have him hit 300 times with a rod on the bridge in the main square. And should I fail to hold my vow, I shall be held accountable and I hereby put my thumbprint so that this is acknowledged by everybody and in any trial court.

May 22nd

"I, Radu Murgan, wrote this to Văsii, the school teacher" (i.e Vasile Hoban around 1690)

Margin note on page 226:

"I, Toma, Chancery writer from...wrote..."

Margin note on page 273:

"I, Vâlcu, the Chancery writer, wrote that God may redeem my father, Anani...Amen and I hereby announce that ...for his *moltiva [old Romanian for* a special prayer*]* Amen"

Margin note on page 315:

"As a record of salvers: 30 salvers and 30 copper platters from boyar Iane; 2 tin 8 copper salvers from zugravu [Romanian for *painter*]; from boyar Mihai Năstăpăritul 50 50 tin salvers, platters (of tin and 40 salvers)".

Margin note on page 315:

"Floarea, son of Todoran"

Margin note on the back cover:

"I, Sta(n)ciul brother Todor wrote this"

"Văsii added to the praise", in Slavonic

3. *FEBRUARY MENAION*

Slavonic manuscript, 144 pages, 31 x 20 cm, wooden and leather binding, inventory no. 9.

Margin note on page 44 in Slavonic:

"...experience the scripture, as Daniel, the visionary, urges. I, Ioan, the Chancery writer inscribed this".

Margin note on page 144:

"This book is purchased by Iuga, God's servant, for the redemption of his soul and donated to the holy church in Şchei, nearby Brasov town, in 7119 (1611) April, the 1st. After that, Radu Voievod, son of Mihnea, was beheaded".

Margin note in Slavonic on the wooden back side of the front cover:

"I, priest Oprea, from the holy church in Şchei"

"May it be known that the date of this inscription by Dumitru, priest in Turcheş"

"it dates back to 7151 (1643)"

Margin note in the Romanian language on the inside of the wooden back cover:

"I, Stoica, wrote this"

Margin note in Slavonic

"I, Vlacu (Valcu), a Chancery writer and son of priest Gheorghe from the holy church in Şchei, nearby Braşov town, wrote this in 7160 (1652), March, the 2nd."

4. *MARCH AND APRIL MENAION*

Manuscript from late 16th century- beginning of the 17th century provided by the library of protopope Mihai, 258 pages, 27.5 x 20 cm, wooden and leather binding, 27 lines per page, inventory no. 11.

Margin notes in Slavonic on the back side of the wooden front cover:

"I, Vasilachi, protopope Vasile, wrote this"

"I, Vasilac, son of protopope Vasile from Braşov, wrote this on March the 4th, 7160 (1652)".

"I, Teodor, son of priest Florea, wrote this"

"I, Vâlcu, son of priest Gheorghe from Braşov, wrote this on April the 23rd."

"I, Teodor, son of priest Florea from Braşov, wrote this on 1711, March the 1st."

"I, Dumitru, son of protopope Petcu, from Turcheş "

Margin notes in Slavonic on the inside of the wooden back cover:

"This book by the name of Menaion belongs to the church in 7119 (1611)"

"I, Vâlcu, son of the priest Gheorghe from Braşov, wrote this on April the 23rd, 7167 (1659)"

"I, Vasilache, son of protopope Vasilie from Braşov, wrote this on March the 8th in 7160 (1652)".

5. *JANUARY MENAION IN SLAVONIC*

Manuscript from the 17th century, 333 pages, 31 x 21 cm., wooden and ornamented leather binding, inventory no. 24.

Margin note in the Romanian language on the back side of the front cover:

"I, Todor, wrote to Mr. Jupan"

Margin note in the Romanian language on page 133:

"May it be known that I, Vasilache, son of Vasilievici from the holy church in Şchei, wrote this on January the 1st, 7160 (1652)",

Margin note in Slavonic:

"This book comes from Putna, Moldova"

Margin note in the Romanian language:

"May it be known that I, Văsiu, son of Hoban and vicar choral in the church from Şchei wrote this in 7159 (1651)",

Margin note in Slavonic:

"Pătru, vicar choral and son of the priest Iane"

Margin note in the Romanian language:

"May it be known that I, Valcu, vicar choral and son of priest Gheorghe from the holy church in Şchei, wrote this on January the 13th, 7161 (1653)",

Margin note in Slavonic:

"I, Micul, from the holy church in Şchei, 1697".

Margin note in Slavonic on the wooden back cover:

"I, Matei, son of priest Oprea from the church in Şchei, 1697".

6. *SLAVONIC RITUAL*

Manuscript dating back to the 17th century, 217 pages, leather and wooden binding, 27.5 x 17 cm, inventory no. 16.

Margin note in the Romanian language on pages 46–49:

"In the name of the Father, the Son and Holy Spirit, amen. I, Grigorie Disstanija Kronsnopolski, God's servant, my wife Maria and my sons ordered this book by the name of Ritual at our expense and donated it to Mihai Ditica, priest in the church of the Holy Resurrection of Jesus Christ, our Redeemer. And should there be anyone who takes this book away from the church, that person shall be cursed and anathema, Amen."

Margin note in the Romanian language on the back side of the front cover:

"I, Staicu, son of priest Staicu from Braşov wrote this in 7198, that is 1690 Anno Domini".

Margin note in the Romanian language on page 1:

"According to David, man's days are like grass and our days are like a passing shadow. I, Avram, archdeacon in the Mitropoly of Bălgard wrote this in 1692 Anno Domini, October the 16th.

7. *CHRONICA DES UNGARISCHEN REICHES*

A three part printing in Nuremberg 1603, 583 pages, the first 26 pages missing, leather and cardboard binding, inventory no. 660.

Cover I in Latin:

"Ex Libris Ioh. Cristian. Posidet. Georg. Christiani. An 1730 die 12 Februar"

Margin note in Latin on page 27:

"Ex Libris B. Baiul (escu)".

8. *MAY MENAION IN SLAVONIC*

Manuscript dating back to 1612, 166 pages, 28.5 x 19 cm, 22 line per page, leather and wooden binding, inventory no. 15.

Margin note in Slavonic on page 2:

"This book dates back to 7120 (1612), May the 1st"

Margin note on page 166 în limba slavonă:

"May the 1st, 7120–1612 Anno Domini, Friday. Devoutly worshipping, I, boyar Drăghici, the courtier".

9. *SLAVONIC RITUAL*

Manuscript dating back to 1610, 327 pages, 25 x 18,5 cm, leather and wooden binding, inventory no. 8.

Margin note in the Romanian language on pages 16–22:

"This book entitled Ritual is ordered by Aghia, the second Treasurer of Moldova, and donated to the church in Şchei whose titular saint is Saint Nicholas the miracle performer, in the Hungarian Country that is below the citadel of Braşov, as an alms gift and so that my name is written in the commemorative list read during the Holy Liturgy. Year 7118 (1610), April the 15th".

10. *APOSTLE'S HOMILY*

Printed in Kiev 1603, 816 pages, 32.7 x 21.3 cm, leather and wooden binding, inventory no. 100.

Margin note in the Romanian language on the back side of cover I:

"May it be known that I, Corbe, wrote this" (i.e. David Corbea who brings the book from Russia).

Added page with a margin note in the Romanian language:

"This book, titled Apostle's Homily, was donated by our holy Metropolitan and father, Chir Ghenadie; Archbishop of all Ardeal, etc. And he gave it to the holy church in Şchei, that is in the suburb, so that the souls of God's servants Pavel and Voica are eternally commemorated and if someone takes it out even if it is for reading purposes only, that person shall be cursed by the Holy Trinity and the saints from Nicaea; and this book should not be sold as long as the holy church endures."

September 7141 (1632)".

11. *GOSPEL FOR INSTRUCTION*

Printing dating back to Matei Basarab, at Govora, 1642, 800 pages, inventory no. 1169.

Margin note in the Romanian language on page 69:

"This jewel belongs to Captain Coste and it was purchased by loose pieces and I wrote this during the reign of our empress, Catherine, in February the 4th".

Margin note in the Romanian language on page 422:

"it is only fair to write in good will and not just like any ordinary man even though I wrote Şerban Pop, of Radu Frumuşica from Târgovişte. May it be known that I, Sărban, high ranking boyar, wrote this".

Margin note in the Romanian language on page 432:

"and Ion Copil, high ranking boyar from Târgovişte wrote this".

Margin note in the Romanian language on page 510:

"the honest and faithful boyar, Costandim Catartea, voivode's commandant and beneficiary.....".

Margin note in the Romanian language on page 540:

"May it be known that I, Tudor Cojon from Târgovişte, wrote this in January, 1763".

Margin note in the Romanian language on page 596:

"I, Pop Anghel, guardian of this holy church whose titular saint is Saint Nicholas, wrote this on July the 13th."

Margin note in the Romanian language on page 781:

"May it be known that I, Ion Copil, high ranking boyar dan priest Tudpor wrote this in May 7280 (1772). May it be known that on Thursday at 11 o'clock God sent hail from the sky and the ice pellets were as big as hen eggs and killed people and animals and birds and put down trees in Târgovişte and destroyed vineyards; and something like this has never happened before and this is because of our many sins."

Margin note in the Romanian language on page 788:

"May it be known that I, Urdea pop, servant of Mr. Polkelui Stevico from Targovişte, wrote in this holy book. And I signed here so that it is known what kind of alphabet is used"

12. *ROMANIAN BOOK FOR EDUCATION*

Printed in Iaşi in 1643 during the rule of Vasile Lupu and of metropolitan Varlaam, 6 copies.

Copy I, margin notes in the Romanian language:

"This holy book belongs to me, priest Ştefan Anghelovici from Feldioara, and I bought it for 22 de zloty that came from selling a plot of land belonging to the church and I only added 8 more zloty from my own pocket and I have been using it to this day. Then after my death my successor can further use it on condition that it returns the 8 zloty to my children. Ştefan Anghelovici, rector and Gherasim Anghelovici, vicar choral".

"This holy book was needed by our church from Feldioara and the church sold a ploughed plot of land to Bucur Miron for 22 zloty....and may he peacefully own it along with any other strangers and their relatives, and whoever shall estrange this book will be cursed by the holy fathers and this was done by protopope Nicolae, in eight hundred 32, November the 12th."

Margin note in the Romanian language on page 218:

"I, Cande, the vicar choral, from Racoviţ bought this book".

Copy III, 414 pages, place of origin: Rupea, inventory no. 1608.

Margin note in the Romanian language on page 414:

"This book belongs to me, priest Moisi from Calbor, and was bought for10 zloty, in Calbor, in 1805, February".

Copy IV, 515 pages, inventory no. 2103:

Margin note in the Romanian language on page 3:

"May it be known that this book belongs to me, priest Bucur from Hîrseni and whoever may steal it is cursed by the 300 and 18 holy fathers....to join the devil in the dark and hell's gaols forever after and I, priest Poapa, wrote this with my own hand."

Copy IV, 468 pages, inventory no. 2278:

Margin note in the Romanian language on page 3–15: "...and the nun Anca gave it to me saying that she and priest Lepădat had bought it to donate as alms for their souls, and whoever may be tempted to take it, his soul along with that of his relatives shall reach the same place as Juda's and the souls of those who crucified Jesus Christ and shall be cursed by all the saints whose names are mentioned by this book. Amen. Note made on May the 8th, 1760".

13. *APOSTLE'S HOMILIES*

Printed in Moscow in 1643, 428 pages, 30.2 x 20 cm, title page missing, binding of wood and leather ornamented with stylish geometric shapes, inventory no. 90 It comes from the library of protopope Mihai.

Margin note in the Romanian language on the back side of the front cover:

"The soul of Babia Barbul commands, year 7111(1603)"

"May it be known that it snowed on Good Friday, during the night before Saturday, on Saturday and on Easter, for three days and it snowed in April on the 1st at night and on the 2nd, as well, in 7178 (1670) and I, Văsii Hobanul, protopope with the holy church in Şchei wrote this."

Margin note in Slavonic.

"Vasilache, son of priest Vasile".

Margin note in the Romanian language on the recto of the title cover page:

"May it be known that the Citadel tower collapsed Saturday night at eleven o'clock. I wrote this I, protopope Vasii Ţearcov in Şchei. I wrote this on June the 29th, in 7104 (1596)"

"May it be known that the Feast of the Annunciation was celebrated at Easter time, on Wednesday when dispensation from fasting is granted to all, and I, boyar Hoban Văsii wrote this during the life of protopope Văsii and Mr. Stancu Hoban from Ţerkov in Şchei in July the 25th, 7115 (1667)".

14. *FUNERAL SERVICE BOOK FOR PRIESTS AND DEACONS*

Printed in Tîrgovişte, in 1650 during the rule of Matei Basarb, 52 pages, 2 pages added at the beginning and at the end of the book, 19 lines per page, inventory no. 129.

Margin note in the Romanian language on pages 1–2:

"You shall commemorate Gherghina, Elena, heir of Mihai and Despina Tud(o)r, dweller within the court (year)of Mihail".

Margin note in the Romanian language on the fly leaf of page 1:

"Boyar Mircea, the *logofat,* guided the God beloved and gifted Mihai, the functionary."

C. *LAW ANTHOLOGY*

Printed in Târgovişte in 1652, 4 copies.

Copy I, inventory no. 1171:

"May it be known that the priest Precup of Toadu bought this holy Anthology from priest Mihăilă from Măterăuşu for 55 guilder ...printed in 1652...and if after the death of priest Precup his sons will be in any need, they shall not sell it without the knowledge of the church council, and if the church council does not want to return their money they are free to sell it wherever they want. And it was first bought back from priest Buzduc Toader from Ruşi Bîrgăului and to this end priest Mihăil paid 15 guilders that came from selling one of his father's estates. I, protopope Buzdug, wrote this in the Rus village".

Copy II, 536 pages, leather and wooden binding, inventory no. 445:

"May it be known that this holy Anthology is mine and I inherited it upon the death of my father, the late protopope Florea dan Teodor Băran and I, God's servant, protopope Florea wrote this dan priest Teodor dan protopope Florea from here in1736, June the 20th."

Copy IV, 747 pages, loose parts, inventory no. 2245:

Margin note in the Romanian language on page 1:

"This holy book titled *Law Anthology* was bound through the efforts of the priest Marin serving with the Balnoc church in1730".

Margin note on page 3, below the writing line:

"May it be known that that I, protopope Şerban, bought this holy anthology when the German went into Wallachia and I wrote this in 1738, February the 4th".

Margin note in the Romanian language on page 8:

"This holy anthology belongs to the church from Făgăraş and it was acquired by protopope Petru Popoviciu".

D. *LIST OF THE LIVING AND THE DECEASED*

Slavonic manuscript dated 1665, 9 pages, leather and cardboard binding, 30.5 x 20 cm, inventory no. 42.

Margin note on page 4:

"I, Mitrul, by my full first name Dumitru, son of priest Cîrstei wrote this and I wrote Stancul, son of protopope Staicului so that you keep commemorating Dumitru until 1711.

E. *AUGUST MENAION IN SLAVONIC*

Manuscript dated between 1664 and 1665, 196 pages, leather and cardboard binding, 30 x 20 cm, inventory no. 33.

Margin note in Slavonic on cover I:

"Pătru, son of Gheorghe Făinăbună, from Braşov, August the 8th, 1664".

F. *CHRISTIAN'S AND JEWS'DISPUTE ON MESIAH*

Printed in Kiev before 1673, 44 pages, 19.3 x 16.3 cm, leather and wooden binding, inventory no. 92.

Margin note in the Romanian language on the back side of cover I:

"Niacşa, wife of Consatntin Marcia, daughter of Stoica of Pricup and of Rada passed away on the Pentecost Saturday at night at three o'clock and may she always be commemorated, May the 17th, year Before Christ ...in 1673 Anno Domini".

Margin note in the Romanian language on page 11:

"Barbu Marce passed away at 4 o'clock in the afternoon and may God remember him and be forever commemorated, 7185(1677)".

"Ana Mărcior, the old mother, passed away at 4 o'clock in the morning in 7185 (1677), may God forgive her."

G. *THE BOOK OF THE APOSTLES WRITTEN BY THE MODEL OF THE GREEK APOSTLES*

Printed in Bucureşti in 1683 upon the order and at the expense of Şerban Cantacuzino and metropolitan Teodosie, 178 pages, 27 x 18 cm, 2 copies received from Grînar village, leather and wooden binding, inventory no. 1773 and 1818.

Copy I

Margin note in the Romanian language on page 3:

"This holy book titled The Apostles belonged to the church established by the merchants from Făgăraş and it was bought for the church of Macudorf from Mekendorf by Floarea and her son in law, Ioanşcu, so that they along with their relatives be always commemorated, and may there be no one to dare to estrange this book from the church and should there be, may he be cursed and anathema on behalf of the 318 holy fathers from Niceea, and I, Andrei, school teacher in Făgăraş wrote this in July 1799."

20. *THE GREEK RITUAL*

Printed in Athens in 1685, 24 pages, 29.5 x 20.3 cm, leather and cardboard binding, inventory no. 132.

Margin note in the Romanian language on the last blank page:

"When the Germans went into Wallachia against the Turks and the boyars and monks took refuge here, there was one monk from Câmpina who had this book in loose parts and sold it as a result of his great need to the Holy Church that at the time was under the guidance of Gerasim Adamovici and the latter had it bound; and the priests and vicar chorals in the church from here were: priest Gheorghe Lebor Bodovici; deacon Eustatie Rad Cătană, vicar choral Radu Duma, Toma Ion Lebovici, and Radu was a vicar choral during the reign of Emperor Joseph II, in 1790 B.C., November the 20th".

21. *EPISTLE*

Manuscript that includes excerpts from Homilies, a lot of proverbs from the Book of Common Prayer or from the Synaxarion, edited in 1680, 296 pages, leather and wooden binding, 30.6 x 20 cm, inventory no. 26.

Margin note in the Romanian language on page 37:

"This Epistle was translated form the Serbian language into Romanian at the expense and with the support of boyar Tudor Cupeş, and I... (Illegible handwriting, most likely Văsii Hoban) son of Văsii, the protopope from the church from Şcheai. Văsiu Hoban".

Margin note in the Romanian language on page 160:

"May it be known that in 1775 it started snowing in October the 14th and the winter was a heavy one. And in spring, in April, the windy weather continued until Easter and people got scared and a lot of animals died of hunger because of the heavy wind and snow and I, on account of my illness, stayed with priest Bucur in Negri Boroştianu. And, I, Adam, school teacher from Bran, wrote this on the 11th of April in 1775".

Margin note in the Romanian language on the interior of the back cover:

"May it be known that Vîlcu, son of priest Ghiorghi, passed away on November the 30th, Wednesday night when Saint Andrew, the Apostle, is celebrated, and they buried him on Friday at 2 o'clock and the funeral was attended by known priests like protopope Staicu, priest Oprea and priest văsii Răuţ, as well as by people. Văsii Hoban and priest Gerghianul from Tohan and priest Ion from there during the time of our functionary Gheorghe Draud and the rule of Mihai Apafz. And I, priest Văsii Hoban, wrote about this on the 1st of December in 1682".

"May it be known that cousin Văsii, son of Comşa Răuţ, the church administrator, passed away – may God forgive him- on Tuesday at around 10 o'clock in the morning, on the 29th of September, 7194 B.C.,1685 A.D. and we buried him in church on Wednesday with due funeral honors and the priests were Candu from Satulung and Dumitru from Târlungeni and Răud Marcul from Ariujd; and this was during the rule of Mihail Apafz and the functionary of Braşov was boyar Ghioghiu and the protopope was Staicul; and I, priest Văsii Hoban, wrote this".

22. *THE HOLY GOSPEL IN ROMANIAN AND GREEK*

Book printed in Bucureşti in 1693 during the rule of Brâncoveanu and the time of metropolitan Tedosie. 470 pages, leather and cardboard binding, inventory no. 2438.

Margin note in the Romanian language on the back side of page:

"Whoever bought and donated this holy Gospel to the church of Prepeuţului, may this be as alms for their souls and may I, monk Ştefan Colţ from Lisnău, writing this, be forever commemorated. 1790, July 23.

"1811 February 19. This Holy Gospel was bought by Aron of Aron on behalf of the church from Prepeuţului whose titular saint is Saint Paraschiva and for his contribution to the church may he and his relatives be forever commemorated. This Holy Gospel was bought by the above mentioned for 15 German coins from priest Nicolae Popovici rector of Zagon as alms for the commemoration of Nicolae Aron Florea and all his relatives. Ioan Seceleanu, Gheorghe Aneşianu, church administrator,

Ioana Bogdan, school teacher, Zagon I witnessed the purchase of this Holy Gospel."

Margin note in the Romnaian language below the last line pages 4–13:

"This Holy Gospel was donated as alms to the holy church from Lisnău by monk Ştefan Colţ and no one should dare to estrange it from the holy church. And whoever may dare to do that shall be under the curse of the Apostles and of the seven Councils. 1790 B.B., July 23, Pop Vlad Popovici. And every priest serving in this church should hold as his duty to commemorate the name of monk Ştefan as one of the church founders".

23. *THE HOLY GOSPEL*

Printed in Snagov in 1697 during the rule of Constantin Brâncoveanu and metropolitan Teodosie, 2 copies:

Copy I-177 pages, 27x18.5cm, inventory no. 2609.

Margin notes in the Romanian language below the text on pages 1–20:

"This holy book titled Gospel I, ...son of...Bundeal *logofat*, bought for 380 Lei but many Christians helped me as much as they could to raise the money and may this be as alms for their souls' commemoration; therefore, for the efforts they made, as long as God allows me to serve as a priest, it is my duty to commemorate the following names during the Liturgy: Costea, Stanciu, Antonie, Mihalcea, Dumitru; and any of my sons or any other relative of mine or any other person shall have this name in commemoration to the end of time ...It is I, priest Oprea, who wrote this in January, 7207(1699)".

Copy II, 79 pages, inventory no. 1599, leather and wooden binding, found in Tîrlungeni.

Margin note in the Romanian language on page 79:

"May it be known that I, Pop Dumtru, wrote this holy Gospel at the expense of dan Oprea Boghici who donated it as alms for his parents' and his own soul. 7023–1722 B.C. 1722 A.D. November the 29th ....".

Margin note in the Romanian language on the last page:

"May it be known that I, Pop Dumitru from Budila, was in love with a soldier subordinated to a captain by the name of by the name of Martin"

24.a. KYRIACODROMION OR GOSPEL FOR EDUCATION

Printed in Alba Iulia in 1699 in two copies:

Copy I, 415 pages, inventory no. 1590.

Margin note in the Romanian language on the fly leaf 1:

"This book of Homilies belongs to the Greek Catholic church from Cincu Mare, December the 1st, 881, C. Mandocea, Greek Orthodox educator in 1881/2".

Margin note in the Romanian language below the text on page 3:

"May it be known that this document belongs to priest Vasile from Calboru and whoever may be tempted to steal it that shall be anathema?"

Copy II, 415 pages, inventory no. 1602:

"In 1801 when I left the Zablău monastery and went for studies to Făgăraş ...and I was 13 of age when I started my education, the teacher was priest Nicolae. Bogrogozi was also a vicar in the Făgăraş bishopric, and I, Sechel Ioan, wrote this with my own hand in Făgăraş".

Margin note in the Romanian language on page 34:

"There was great commotion in the Austrian Empire in 1848."

24.b. September 14th MENAION

Printed in Buzău in 1698 in two copies:

Copy I, 152 pages, bound together with the October Menaion that bears the same title page, leather and wooden binding, inventory no. 94.

Margin note in the Latin alphabet on page 152:

"And I, Barbu Petrescu, wrote this in April, 1808."

Copy II, very damaged with a lot of missing pages, and the rest of the pages are loose, inventory no. 1589.

25.a. GUIDING BOOK WITH TEACHINGS FROM THE EASTERN ORTHODOX DOGMAS TO SERVE AGAINST THE SEPARATION PREACHED BY THE CATHOLICS

Printed in Snagov in 1699 by Antim Ivireanu, 108 pages, 20 x15 cm, inventory no. 33.

Margin note in the Romanian language on page 108:

"May it be known that this book is mine, Teodor HAGI Radul (i.e. Bighici), August 21, 1783, Braşov",

"May it be known that I, Pop the *logo(făt)*, a relative of boyar Hagi Radu Boghici, wrote this in 7260 (1753)",

"The relegation of Constantin Vodă (i.e. Brâncoveanu) was dispatched the 24th of March, the Wednesday during the Holy Week, at 6 o'clock in the afternoon; the next day at 9 o'clock in the morning Şerban Cantacuzino is nominated ruler in 7222 (1714) and on Friday at 9 o'clock Constantin Vodă along with all his sons and sons in law is taken to the Ottoman Court, and that is good news for everybody. And I, Preda, copilul (Romanian for *the child*), wrote this while taking courses to become a school teacher"

25.b. NOVEMBER AND DECEMBER MENAION

Printed in Buzău in 1698, 163 pages, wooden binding, inventory no. 95.

Margin note in the Romanian language on page 2:

"Tempianu 1781".

Margin note in the Romanian language on the inside of Cover 2:

"On the 11th of December, 1750, triplets are christened on the same day, one by the name of Ioan, another by the name of Radu, and a third one called Stoica and their parents are from the old part of Braşov town".

26. JANUARY MENAION

Printed in Buzău in 1698, 187 pages, leather and wooden binding, inventory no. 96.

Margin note in the Romanian language on page 187:

"this Menaion was bound for the second time through the insignificant effort of God's sinful servant Radul dan Tempea, Scheai Braşov, in our parents' and our commemoration. 1727, December 31".

27. FEBRUARY MENAION

Printed in Buzău, In 1689, 200 pages, inventory no. 97.

Margin note IN THE Romanian language on page 2:

"This Menaion was bound for the second time through the insignificant effort of the hereby signatories in commemoration of our names and of our parents, in 1727, January the 31st. Radu Tempea from the holy church in Şchei Braşov".

"God's hidden mysteries are hard to decipher during a man's life time, but God's miracles need to be made known to all those who are willing to understand them. In 1731, March the 1st, by God's will, a most precious document was discovered in the church in Schei whose titular saunt is Saint Nicholas the Miracle Performer, located near Braşov, in the Bîrsa County. This holy church has been mercifully supported by the late Petru

Vo(evod) also called Cercel, ruler of Moldova, the one who contributed to the building of the six pillars in the church portico, also called *Peritfor*, as well as by the late Aron vodă up until Gerge Ştefan Voievod. And that document was not to be found between 7164 (1656)–7239(1731), and we wondered when it was discovered. And upon everybody's advice we found the saint and priest Teodor son of Proto(pop)e Floria and sent it to Iaşi, in Moldova, to his Highness, the blessed ruler Grigore Ghica Voevode. And with the support of the boyars related to the voivode and with God's mercy, the holy church got back the document by the will of Grogorie Voevode The Merciful One, a merciful and forever commemorated ruler, during the time of Protopope Floria B(ăran)i,priest Radu Tempia, and priest Teodor Băran, priest Staie Grid on the 15th of August, 1731. Pop Teodor son of Floria (Băran) of place from where I wrote this".

A chronicle like margin note in the Romanian language on page 3:

"February the 21st, 1699"

The enlightened and faithful Christian, on whom God has shed his mercy and who dearly loves holy churches and makes efforts to have God bless and save him and his family's souls and who now is happily living. The above mentioned fortunate Christian ruler, Ioan Constantin Bră/ncoveanu/băsărab/Voe/vode after having made many donations to the holy church in Schei, near the Braşov Citadel, whose titular saint is Saint Nicholas and that celebrates the Assumption of Virgin Mary, this most merciful and holy voivode gave 12 Menaions covering the 12 months of the year to this church. May God receive his alms in the afterlife and may his Highness long live in peace and good health, and may he rule and be blessed along with his family until he reaches old age, and may he enter the God's kingdom of light and green where all saints are and where we all wish to reach; and when he made this donation I was a priest in the above mentioned church. The first priest serving here was protopope Văsii dan protopope Vasii Hoban, the second – Văsii Grid, the third Carstea dan priest Stancul, the fourth –priest Floria dan Todoran Băran (and the first church administrator during this times was Stoica Postăvariul, followed by Ghorgşi Vătafu), and Boyar Stan Toan (i.e. Soan), a member of his Highness court, was the one who made efforts to bring books, may God forgive his parents and give him good health. And I, protopope Văsii Hobanovici, wrote this so that God may strengthen him and forgive and show His mercy towards us forever after Amen".

28. APRIL AND MARCH MENAION
Printed in Buzău in 1698, 224 pages, inventory no. 98.
Margin note in the Romanian language on fly leaf I:
"Ex Ecclesiae Bolgareschia"
Margin note in Latin alphabet on page 1:
"Tiodor Raduli, year 1781, December".

29. JUNE MENAION
Printed in Buzău in 1698, 160 pages, inventory no. 1615.
Margin note in the Romanian language on the last fly leaf:
"This menaion was bound by Grid Radovici Dimitrie, 1779, October 16th "
Margin note in the Romanian language on the fly leaf.
"I, Stan from Huşi, wrote here on this holy book in September ...the 12th and my hand is of dust and will rot long after similar to 118 years ago when Rafail from Huşi, in his turn, wrote here."
Margin note in the Romanian language on page 150:
"I, Adam Caţavei, school teacher in Făgăraş, served for many years in the church in Union with the Roman Catholic Church under 5 vicars, as follows: Ioan Para, Ioan Helenghie and Dumitru Costa, Constantin Alemas, Teodor Senii al 5-lea.
In 843 June the 27th, Adam Caţavei, was a school teacher of Făgăraş and in 846 Ioan Kerilă from Blaj comes as a vicar".
Margin note in the Romanian language on the page before the last:
"May there be known that in 1843, April the 24th the priest Ghoeghe Moldovean from Făgăraş went to the Nicula monastery. 1843, April the 24th,Adam Caţavei in Racoviţă".
Margin note in the Romanian language on the last page before the fly leaf :
"In 1843, June the 4th, our Emperor Ferdinand and all the high ranking officials of Transylvania were willingly appointed in this province of the Austro Hungarian Empire".

B. Names of People Recorded in the Margin notes

1. ORTHODOX ROMANIAN PRIESTS FROM SCHEI

H. Names of people recorded in the margin notes

Mihai I (1578–1604)
Son of priest Dobre, last descendent of the family, is a school educator in Schei. He attends the Serbian school from Pec. He is anointed priest in Râşnov and serves as such between 1576 and 1578. He is a priest and protopope in Braşov between 1578 and1605. He donated most of the manuscripts to be found in the Schei archive. He is a collaborator of Coresi and makes his house available for the activities of a school of copyists. As a school teacher he makes the effort to erect the stone building from Schei. He has two sons: Constantin and Vasile.

Balea
Priest in Şchei between 1591 and1595.

Neagoslav
Priest in Şchei between 1595 and1606. He comes from Târgul de Floci to Şchei upon the recommendation of Michael the Brave.

Constantin
Son of Mihai I, priest in Şchei between 1605 and1628.

Vasile II (1586–1659)
The youngest son of protopope Mihai and school teacher in Şchei as of 1604. He records in his chronicle the moment when Michael the Brave goes through Braşov. In 1628, when he is appointed rector, hemakes a donation in books from his father's library. In 1611 he facilitates and records the donation made by boyar Iuga to the church in Şchei. From a cultural point of view, he authors the first chronicle in the Romanian language, which is a complete history of the the Church of Saint Nicholas. He dies in 1659 and is buried in the church portico.

Stanciu Hoban
There are two branches of this family. In 1598, one of these branches is represented by Stan and Dumitru Hoban, dwelling in the Ciocrac area (in Şchei). Between 1613 and 1634 the other branch is represented bz the first

decsendent, Stanciu Hoban, dwelling in the Tocile neighborhood in Şchei. The latter is a school teacher in Şchei and then a priest and has a clash with priest Vâlcu. He dies in 1681 and has only one heir, Vasile Hoban.

Vâlcu
Vasile Oltean dates his presence back to 1659, whereas Muşlea only shows him after 1661 until November 1682. He is known for his plots that lead to tensions between the priests in Şchei and the magistrate of Braşov. He is the son of priest Gheorghe, who also served in Şchei.

Oprea I (Chipria)
He serves as a priest in Satulung until 1671, and between 1671 and 1692 as a priest in Şchei. He has a son by the name of Matei.

Staicu I
He serves as a priest in the Turcheş village before 1671, and between 1671 and 1690 as a protopope in Şchei. He has a son who bears his first name.

Vasile Hoban
Son of Staicu Hoban, priest and copyist, school teacher with the school in Şchei between 1659 and 1680.

Ioan Corbea
Son of merchant Florea Corbea. Like his father, he acts as a school teacher and diplomat in Braşov. He dispatches numerous messages to Wallachia and Moldova. He serves as a priest in the Church of Saint Nicholas between 1659 and 1661. After the death of his wife, he takes the oath as a monk and from hereon is named Iosif and serves in the monastery from Sinaia. He has two sons, David andTeodor Corbea.

Văsii Hoban
Son of Vasile Hoban, school teacher in Şchei as of 1685, and priest and protopope with the Church of Saint Nicholas as of 1697.

Vasile Comşa Răuţ
Between 1680 and 1685 he serves as a priest in Tohan and then in Şchei. He has a son who is a church administrator. His burial is recorded in one of the margin notes.

Vasile Grid (1686–1747)
He comes to Şchei from Făgăra and acts as a priest between 1686 and 1717. He has a son, Eustatie.

Cîrstea (Christianus I)
School teacher with the school in Şchei, son of protopope Staicu. As of 1687 he is a deacon and then a priest in Şchei starting in 1691 until 1716. He has a son by the name of Mitru, mentioned by a margin note.

Teodor
Deacon of the church in 1691, dies shortly afterwards in Bucureşti.

Florea Băran
Son of merchant Teodor Băran, in Şchei. School teacher before 1692, and then he is anointed and serves as a priest until 1717, and then as a protopope. He has a son, Teodor Băran.

Radu Tempea I (?- 1713)
He comes to Braşov from Făgăraş and is related to protopope Staicu. He serves as a deacon in Şchei and then as a protopope between 1699 and 1713.

Radu Tempea II
Son of Radu Tempea I and serves as a deacon in Şchei between 1713 and 1716, as a priest between 1716–1735 and as a protopope between 1735–1742. He is the author of *Istoria Sfintei bisearici a Şcheilor Braşovului* (*The History of the Holy Church in Şchei, Braşov*) and fights for the rights of the Orthodox Romanians.

Teodor Băran
Son of Florea, attends the school in Şchei and then continues his studies in Râmnic and Câmpulung. He returns home as a school teacher in Şchei. Between 1713 and in 1717 he serves as a church deacon and as a priest between 1717 and 1742.

Eustatie Grid (1721–1767)
Son of protopope Vasile Grid, school teacher in Şchei and then a priest and protopope between 1721 and1742.

Petcu (Petru) Şoanul
School teacher and priest in Şchei between 1735 and 1741.

Radu Tempea III (1720–1763)
School teacher working with the school in Şchei, nominated deacon in July 1741, in Bucureşti, and anointed priest in Serbia 1742 by Todor, the patriarch. Upon the orders of the magistrate from Braşov he is imprisoned along with his father for having defended the position of the Romanian Orthodox. In 1746 he is mentioned as the fifth priest, of the six serving with the Şchei church.

Adam Caţavei
Priest from Făgăraş who comes to Braşov, where he serves in 1843.

2. ORTHODOX ROMANIAN PRIESTS FROM AROUND BRAŞOV

There is one mention in particular that needs to be made from the very beginning concerning the list of priests from around Braşov. It does not include the complete dates on their activity since they are not mentioned in any other documents. However, this list is important for the current study because it adds to the number of people who are already known for their activity around the church in Şchei.

Dumitru
Priest in Turcheş village in 1611.

Petcu
Priest in Turcheş village in 1699. He has a son, Dumitru.

Dumitru Ghorghianu
Priest in Tohan vilalge in 1682 he a participates along with Ioan, a priest in Tohan, at Vâlcu's funeral).

Candu
Priest in Satulung in 1685.

Dumitru
Priest in Târlungeni in 1685.

Răud Marcul
Priest in Aiujd in 1685.

Dumitru
Priest in Boiu village in 1669.

Dumitru
Priest in Budila in 1722.

Marin
Priest in Banloc in 1730.

Şerban
Protopope of Braşov in 1738.

Stan and Rafael
Priests in a church from Huşi, before 1779.

Ştefan Colţ
Monk in Lisnău, in 1790.

Vlad Popovici
Priest in Lisnău in 1790.

Nicolae Bodrugazi
Priest in the Făgăraş bishopric in 1801.

Moise
Priest in Calbor (near Făgăraş).

Farcaş
Priest in Ticuş village la 1829.

Ştefan Anghelovici
Priest in Feldioara in 1832.

Ioan Moldovan
Priest in Racoviţa village, near Făgăraş in 1843.

Vasile
Priest in Calbor village between 1881 and 1882.

Mihăilă
Priest in Măterăuş village in 1870.

Buzduc
Priest and protopope in Ruşii Bârgăului village.

Petre Popovici
Protopope of the Greek Orthodox Church from Făgăraş

Ioan Petric
Protopope of Braşov.

3. SCHOOL TEACHERS AND COPYISTS

It is worth noting that the school teachers in Şchei, also served as priests in this neighborhood. Consequently, most of them are listed among the names of the priests'. in Şchei.

Toma, the Chancery writer
His name is recorded along with that of Petre Pop şi Stoica Negul in the accounting books of Braşov. As a child, he is a domestic in the house of Craiova's ruler, then a *logofăt* and interpreter for the magistrate of Braşov. He acts as messenger on behalf of the Saxons in the Wallachian courts. He takes the oath as a monk on the 21st of May 1572 and divides his fortune among his children.

Ioan Pisariu
Son of protopope Petre from Turcheş, a Chancery writer in Şchei in1611.

Dimitrie Grid Eustatievici
Son of Eustatie Grid. he is sent to attend school in Moscow in 1743. He authors *Gramatica româneasca* (*Romanian Grammar*) which he dedicates to the Wallachian ruler Constantin Mavrocordat (a copy of it can be found in the Şchei archive). In 1796 he is nominated director of National Schools.

Eustatie Radu Cătană
Church deacon who comes from a family of merchants in Şchei. In 1796, he copies for the further use of the school from this neighborhood *Istoria câtorva împăraţi romani* (*A History on Some Roman Emperors*). He has a son by the name of Eusatie Cătană.

Radu Dimitrie Duma
School teacher in Şchei and teacher of music. He acts as a deputy of the abbot and monastery administrator. The first representative of the family whose name is mentioned acts as a church administrator in 1772, and Dimitrie Duma becomes protopope in Trei Scaune and then in Braşov. In

1775 he dies of plague, an epidemic that spreads in Braşov. He has a son by the name of Ioan Duma.

Stoica Postăvarul and Gheorghe Vătafu
Church administrators of the church in Şchei in 1731.

Mandocea Constantin
Greek Orthodox school teacher in Cincu Mare in 1881–1882.

4. OTHER NAMES

Ghedanie de Brad
Metropolitan of Ardeal (17 October 1627–September 1640).

Teodosie
Metropolitan of Wallachia (25 April, 1668–1672 for the first time, and for the second time starting with 26 April 1679 until 27 January 1708).

Mitrofan
Bishop of Buzău (September 1716–1719).

Avram
Archdeacon and metropolitan of Bălgrad in 1692.

Gherasim Adamovici
Orthodox bishop of Buda, Câmpia Mihaciului and Ardeal (1789–1796).

Iuga Pojar
Boyar from Wallachia. At the beginning of the 17th century he takes refuge in Braşov since he is a member of the group of boyars who betray ruler Radu Mihnea (1611–1612).

Teodor Boul
The second treasurer of Moldova in 1610.

Şerban Pop (Bujoreanu)
Son of Dima Bujoreanu from Olăneşti and of Tudora, brother in law of Ivaşcu Băleanu, son of Pătru Băleanu. He is an equerry in 1679, *logofăt* and treasurer in 1681, High Treasurer between 1704 and1714. He is a Caimacam of Nicolae Mavrocordat until the latter arrives in the country (1716). He takes the side of those favoring the Empire and takes refuge in Transylvania in 1718. He has two sons: Răducanu and Preda.

Mihai veljudeț

Most likely, Mihai Calofeanu (from Coțofei and from Țânțăreni). He is the son of Preda țânțăreanu, Lord Steward, and of his wife, Mare, nephew (niece?) of Nuacșei, sister of Șeran, Lord Steward in 1628. He takes refuge in Transylvania along with Matei Basarab until 1632. He is High Steward during the latter's rule, as well as High Spatharus between 1624 and 1635.

Gheorghe Stoica

From Crihalma, founder.

Tudor Hagi Radu (Boghici)

The researcher A. Mureșianu states the following: The Boghici family comes from the Doicești and Rudeni families of boyars. Dan Constantin Doicești Brașoveanu, a merchant, is married to Pătru alița, daughter of Chiriță Doicescu, the cupbearer, son of Radu Doicescu, the cupbearer and of Ilinca. The latter is the daughter of Radu Rudeanu and mother of Ioan and Constantin Boghici in 1791. These two either make donations or print books for the church in Șchei. Todor Boghici is the first member of this family mentioned in church records (Dumitru and Oprea Boghici are also mentioned in 1686). Between 1697 and 1698, during the time of Constantin Brâncoveanu, there is a man by the name of Ioan Boghici, a butcher, who lives in Schei, Brașov. In 1724 in the allegiance made by the priests in Șchei to uphold the Orthodox faith and the Orthodox church, one of the signatories is somebody by the name of Oprea Boghici. The family was in commerce and their import-export business of Radu and Ioan Boghici was one of the most important of the 132 commercial firms recorded in Brasov in 1769. Constantin Boghi is the last descendant of this family whose name is recorded in 1810.

Gheorghe Făinăbună

Merchant from Șchei, signatory of deeds between Brâncoveanu and the merchants in Șchei. He had a son, Pătru, who worked as a school teacher in Șchei, in 1664.

The Marcea Family

Known from a commemorative list: Ana Mărcior, the grandmother dies in 1677, along with barbu Marce; Neacsa, wife of Constantin Marcea and daughter of Stoica Precup and Rada from Şchei, who dies in 1673.

Gheorghe Bălan and Borgo Rusu

Cantors in the Ruşii Bârgăului village in 1870.

C. Alphabetical Index of Places Mentioned in Book Annotations

Balnoc, in Harghita county.

Budila, near Braşov.

Bundad-Bund, Boiu near Sighişoara.

Bungar, near Sibiu.

Calboru or Calbonu, Beclean township near Făgăraş.

Cincu Mare, near Braşov.

Crihalma, near Braşov.

Feldioara, nearBraşov.

Hârseni, near Făgăras.

Husi, in Vaslui county.

Lisnău, nearTârgu Secuiesc.

Monastery of Nicula, near Cluj. It is established in 1695 and its wooden church hosts the icon of Virgin Mary. In 1772 there is only one monk serving here and it depends on the bishopric of Gherla that is in Union with the Roman Catholic Church.

Măterăus, Magherus, near Târgu Secuiesc.

Racovita, monastery. The small nunnery from here was built by the monk Oprea Doican on his own estate. In 1769 it is recorded as a monastery in the Union with the Roman Catholic Church.

Satu Lung, near Brasov.

Toadu, near Brasov.

Ticus, near Rupea.

Tîrlungeni, near Brasov.

Turches, near Brasov.

Viştea de Jos, near Făgăras.

Zablău, in Covasna county.